MY ANCEST(
A GENTLEMAN

by Stuart A. Raymond

SOCIETY OF GENEALOGISTS ENTERPRISES LTD.

Published by
Society of Genealogists Enterprises Limited
14 Charterhouse Buildings, Goswell Road
London EC1M 7BA.

ISBN: 978-1-907199-16-5

British Library Cataloguing in Publication Data.
A CIP Catalogue record for this book is available from the British Library.

The Society of Genealogists Enterprises Limited is a wholly owned
subsidiary of the Society of Genealogists, a registered charity, no 233701.

About the Author

Stuart Raymond studied history and politics at Keele University, and submitted a thesis based on Cornish probate records for his Adelaide University MA. He also studied librarianship at the College of Librarianship Wales. After a spell as librarian of the Yorkshire Archaeological Society, he spent many years as an academic librarian in Australia before returning to the UK in 1990. Since then, he has published numerous genealogical bibliographies, directories of genealogical websites, and other handbooks for genealogists. Stuart is a partner in the Family History Partnership, who recently published his *The Home Front 1939-45: a guide for family historians* (2012). Another recent publication is *The wills of our ancestors: the family and local historian's guide to probate records* (Pen & Sword, 2012). This is his second book in the present series; his first was *My ancestor was an apprentice* (2010). Currently, he is working on a guide to the contents of the parish chest, and on updating some of his web directories. **www.stuartraymond.co.uk**

CONTENTS

List of illustrations

Acknowledgements

I am much indebted to Else Churchill at the Society of Genealogists for her encouragement and advice as this book progressed. One of my Pharos students, Mark O'Meara, kindly read an early draft and made some useful suggestions. The illustration of the Bourchier hatchment was supplied and commented on by David Oates, formerly of the University of Exeter. Most of the other illustrations are taken from Wikimedia. **http://commons.wikimedia.org/wiki/Main_Page**.

CHAPTER ONE
Introduction

The aim of this book, as with others in the series, is to suggest ways in which you can trace your ancestors, in this case focusing upon the upper crust of society. The first chapter places the English and Welsh landed gentry in their historical context; subsequent chapters describe and discuss the various techniques and sources which can be used to trace them. Heraldic records are obviously important for the gentry in a way that they are not for most other groups. Title deeds and other estate records are also vital, especially the family and marriage settlements by which gentle families provided for the descent of their estates. The records of taxation and other impositions may also reveal valuable information, as may a number of other sources. Many gentlemen's sons entered professions such as the church, the army, and the law. The records of these professions have been considered in detail elsewhere. In this book, I have tried to provide brief outlines of what is available, and point you to where you can find further information (much of which is available in other books in this series).

I have not covered here some of the major sources which must be used by all genealogists. Parish registers are obviously important for tracing gentry baptisms, marriages and burials, but I have already discussed them in depth in my *Parish registers: a history and guide* (Family History Partnership, 2009). The census and civil registration are also important for the nineteenth and twentieth centuries; they are fully described in my *The Census 1801-*

1

1911: a guide for the internet era (Family History Partnership, 2009), and in my *Civil registration* (Family History Partnership, forthcoming). Trade directories are as important for the gentry as they are for those below them in the social scale; they have been explored in *Directing the past: directories and the local historian,* edited by Gareth Shaw (British Association for Local History, 2003)[1]. Further discussion of these sources would be superfluous.

The prime focus of this book is on the period between the sixteenth and the nineteenth century, although there will be some discussion of their origins, and some important later sources will be mentioned. It was during this period that the gentry flourished, and helped to create the sources which will be discussed here.

Further Reading

Genealogy is now a mass hobby. That was not true in the nineteenth century and earlier. The authors of the earliest genealogical textbooks wrote for a gentry audience; consequently, much of the information they provide relates to the gentry. In this regard, the work of Sims has never been surpassed. He provides numerous references to works, both manuscript and printed, which are still likely to be of use in tracing gentle ancestors, but which are rarely mentioned in modern genealogical textbooks. See:

* SIMS, RICHARD. *A manual for the genealogist, topographer, antiquary and legal professor* ... 2nd ed. John Russell Smith, 1861.

1. Portrait of a Gentleman, by Frans Hals (Wikimedia).

CHAPTER TWO

The Gentry

Society has changed dramatically since the nineteenth century. That is reflected in the language we use to talk about our status in society. 'Gentleman' is a term that was once used in an exclusive sense, to refer to people of some wealth and standing in society. Between the fourteenth and the nineteenth century, gentlemen - the gentry - were men who stood just below the nobility in wealth and political power. Since the early twentieth century, 'gentleman' has become a very inclusive term, so much so that its plural abbreviation, 'gents', has become the usual word used for male public toilets. Public speakers frequently begin speaking by addressing 'Ladies and gentlemen'. A gentleman is usually thought of as a man who possesses certain admirable qualities, such as bravery, politeness, honour, and chivalrousness. In the twenty-first century, anyone can be thought of as a gentleman, although there are still vestiges of the original meaning of the term to be found.

Film and television viewers, and the readers of classic literature such as Jane Austen's *Emma* and Flora Thompson's *Lark Rise*, are familiar with an older picture of the gentleman. He was the owner of country mansions and wide acres, who regularly rode to hounds, patronised his tenants, went to London for the season, sent his sons to public school and university, and looked down on those who claimed to be gentlemen but, in his eyes, were not.

The social mores of the gentleman have long been emphasised. They have been seen by some as the means by which a gentleman is to be recognised. Sir William Vaughan, writing in 1626, argued that 'the means to discern a gentleman be these. First, he must be affable and courteous in speech and behaviour. Secondly, he must have an adventurous heart to fight and that but for very just quarrels. Thirdly, he must be endowed with mercy to forgive the trespasses of his friends and servants. Fourthly he must stretch his purse to give liberally unto soldiers and unto them that have need; for a niggard is not worthy to be called a gentleman. These be the properties of a gentleman, which whosoever lacketh deserveth but the title of a clown or of a country boor'[2].

Vaughan painted an ideal picture of how a gentleman should behave. In practice, many gentlemen did not behave like this, but were nevertheless recognised as gentlemen. A more realistic portrait was painted by William Harrison in 1577. In his opinion, 'whosoever studieth the laws of the realm, whoso abideth in the university giving his mind to his book, or, professeth physic and the liberal sciences, or, beside has service in the room of a captain in the wars, or good counsel given at home, whereby his commonwealth is benefited, can live without manual labour, and thereto is able and will bear the port, charge, and countenance of a gentleman, he shall for money have a coat and arms bestowed upon him by heralds, and thereunto being made so good cheap, be called master, which is the title that men give to esquires and gentlemen, and reputed for a gentleman ever after'[3].

Harrison's gentleman was a sixteenth century invention. In the mid fifteenth century, it was thought that 'a man is not called gentle on account of his riches or his wisdom, but solely on account of his warlike prowess in arms'[4]. Even then, however, the profession of arms was in decay; the end of the Hundred Years War marked at least the beginning of the end of the notion that gentility depended on bearing arms in war[5]. Fewer opportunities for soldiering meant that the gentry had to find some other rationale for the existence of their class. Military service continued to provide that rationale in theory, but in practice the gentle classes evolved into landed gentry. In the fifteenth century, lesser landowners were increasingly able to assert their gentle status in defiance of the older tradition. By Tudor times, landowning was usually accepted as a test of gentility, although there were always ambiguities at the margins[6]. It was not until the late sixteenth century that Lord Burleigh could argue that gentility was but ancient riches[7]. Education was also important; Sir Philip Sidney thought that 'You will bee ungentle gentlemen if you bee no schollers'[8].

Between 1500 and 1900, the gentry were very attached to their status, but more concerned with landed estates and local government than with the business of war. Indeed, there were some who denied that they had any business engaging in soldierly activities. Lawyers in particular saw no social distinction between themselves and knights or esquires who went to war. Nevertheless, even in the fifteenth century they could argue that the possession of heraldic arms did not imply that they should go to the wars[9]. The Welsh bards ceased to hymn the martial values of the gentry, but instead concentrated on 'the role of the gentleman as a conscientious magistrate, legally knowledgeable, and administering justice even-handedly'[10]. The country house replaced the castle as the symbol of power.

A gentleman's primary concern was with his landed estates, and his country house. His aim was to ensure that the house and its attached estates descended virtually intact, not just to his immediate heir, but also to his heir and all subsequent heirs, ad infinitum. He had to guard against a wide range of potential threats, such as the problems that could be encountered during minorities, the possibility of wastrel heirs, the demands of the state, especially (before 1646) for feudal dues, and the possibility of litigation against the family. Lawyers developed the concept of the strict settlement to ensure, as far as was humanly possible, that family estates were retained by the family in perpetuity.

Minorities were both a threat and an opportunity. Although a boy aged 14 could consent to marriage, he had to wait until he was 21 before he could manage his own estate[11]. The estate might suffer from the feudal extortions of the Court of Wards. Guardians (known as committees) imposed by the Crown might force heirs to marry unsuitable brides, or demand extortionate fines if they refused to do so[12]. Encroachments on property rights were much more likely during a minority, especially if there was no watchful steward. But an estate that was heavily in debt might benefit from the possibilities of retrenchment that a minority offered[13].

Gentlemen were also concerned to ensure that their houses were designed for living the life of a country gentleman in all its diverse aspects - they needed rooms for administering their estate, for keeping their muniments, for administering justice. They needed libraries for their antiquarian pursuits, lodgings for their servants, stables for their horses, kennels for their dogs, and ballrooms for their dances. A gentleman's country seat was a symbol of the social and economic standing of its owner, and an essential qualification for membership of the local landed elite.

Status was also reflected in a gentleman's household arrangements. He had to have servants. In 1825, it was recommended that a gentleman with a wife and children, and an income of £4000 to £5000 per annum, should have a housekeeper, a cook, a lady's-maid, a nurse, two house-maids, a laundry-maid, a still-room maid, a nursery-maid, a kitchen-maid, and a scullion, with a butler, a valet, a house-steward, a coachman, two grooms, one assistant groom, two footmen, three gardeners, and a labourer[14]. The fact that such staffing was recommended in print is indicative of the importance attached to keeping up with society's expectations.

The gentry were just below the nobility in the heirarchy of society; indeed, the terms 'nobility' and 'gentility' were originally synonymous. The meaning of status terms has altered considerably over the centuries. The word 'gentle' is derived from the Latin for kinsman. It refers, not to blood relations, but to those related by feudal tenure. Feudal lords granted lands to their followers in return for military service. That land was said to be a knight's fee, held by knight service. All who held land by this type of tenure were gentle (although not all were knights). Gentlemen originally derived their status, not from their personal qualities, but from their tenure of land by knight service. They had that in common with the baronage. Before c.1500, there was a much wider gap between the gentry and villeins than there was between barons and the gentry.

In the following centuries, status amongst the elite began to be more differentiated. The barons became more of a separate order, and several ranks developed within the gentry. By the seventeenth century, there was a wide gap between the parish gentleman with a few hundred acres, and the baronet with wide estates in several counties. Writing in 1600, Sir Thomas Wilson suggested that knights 'for the most part are men for living betwixt £1000 and £2000 yearly'; esquires had rents of between £500 and £1000; gentlemen living close to London might have between 1000 marks (£666) and £1000, but 'Northward and far off a gentleman of good reputacion may be content with 300 and 400 yerly'[15]. Shortly after he wrote, James I created the order of baronetcies. In 1642, there were 30 baronets, 70 knights, 256 esquires, and 323 mere gentlemen in Yorkshire[16]. The four ranks who made up the landed gentry had come into being: baronets, knights, esquires, and mere gentlemen.

Baronets were at the summit of the gentry hierarchy. Their creation was a deliberate act of policy by James I, who needed money for his troops in Ireland. The first baronetcies cost their holders £1095. Cash for honours was perfectly respectable in seventeenth-century England; indeed, they were a popular and useful way of moderating demands on the taxpayer. Anyone who could afford to pay the sums demanded (which were soon reduced in order to attract more buyers) was seen as deserving of the increased precedence that possession of the rank gave. The idea that their numbers should be limited to 200 was quickly discarded[17]. In Yorkshire alone, 35 baronets were created between 1611 and 1642. One of the first was Sir William Wentworth of Wentworth Woodhouse, the richest gentleman in the county, who had an income of £6000 per annum. Even he, however, was not attracted to the idea of becoming a peer of the realm - it would have cost him £6000[18].

Knights were next in rank. Unlike the baronets, their origins could be traced back for over half a millenia, to the Anglo-Saxon cnicht, or mounted soldier, who accompanied his war lord to the battlefield. By the twelfth century, the word had become synonymous with the Old French 'chevalerie', from which we derive the word chivalry.

6

Under Norman rule, knights were expected to undertake military service in return for the land they held by knight service. The service due was gradually commuted to a monetary payment known as scutage or shield money. When knights' fees finally disappeared under the Abolition of Tenures Act in 1660, the military service this tenure placed on the landowner had not been demanded for centuries. Nevertheless, knights retained an important role on the battlefield. The Earl of Essex dubbed many knights when he was sent to oppose Irish rebels in the 1590s, much to Queen Elizabeth's annoyance. She thought that most of Essex's knights did not have the requisite wealth to support the dignity.

Below the knight were the esquires. This rank originally marked a stage in the military training of the nobility. Young men began their training as pages, who did not fight. They then became esquires, who accompanied knights to battle, before becoming knights themselves. Some, however, did not advance beyond the rank of esquire. By the fifteenth century, the term began to be applied to the eldest sons of knights. It was also applied to the heralds, to Justices of the Peace, and to certain other officers. In the ensuing centuries, usage of the term steadily widened. The status was gradually assumed by all those 'of some competent quantity of revenue fitt to be called to office and authority in their Country where they live', as Sir Thomas Wilson put it[19]. Esquires, with the knights, were the leading members of county society from the sixteenth century.

At the bottom of the gentry hierarchy was the mere gentleman. The term 'gentleman' was not itself a military term, as the terms 'knight' and 'esquire' were. Gentlemen could not be identified by their military status. That status derived, rather, from their ability to live of their own, without the need to work with their hands. The contemporaries of the future Sir John Rolle were horrified that he was ploughing a Cornish field when he heard the news that he had inherited his cousin's great estates in Devon and Cornwall in 1647[20], His action rendered him suspect in their eyes. His gentlemanly status was not in question, but his ploughing was thought to have been dishonourable. The status of a gentleman depended on common fame that he behaved like gentlemen. If he did not, he was not.

Common fame was an elastic concept. England in the early modern period was a competitive society, with men anxious to achieve status. The numbers of those aspiring to be called gentleman surged during the period, and greatly exceeded the numbers of those who might have been thought of as lesser esquires in the fourteenth and fifteenth centuries[21]. The designation, 'gentleman', like that of 'esquire' became ever wider in its usage. It had originally been limited to the brothers and younger sons of esquires, but was increasingly claimed by minor landowners, professionals such as doctors and lawyers, and wealthier members of urban communities. They thought of themselves as gentry by reason of their birth, their education, their wealth, or simply their social aspirations. Their wealth distinguished them from their neighbours, as did their possession of heraldic arms, or, at least, their right to apply for them. Nevertheless, lesser gentlemen were frequently looked down on by their more established brethren as being not quite gentry. In particular, there was substantial hostility to the idea that wealth generated by trade entitled its owner to gentility. That hostility continued at least until the Victorian era, although it was somewhat moderated by the fact that the sons of gentlemen and tradesmen played cricket together on the fields of Eton, Harrow, and other public schools. Probate records sometimes demonstrate that a man's opinion of his own status was not always shared by his neighbours. Someone who called himself a gentleman in his will may well have been designated 'yeoman', or even 'husbandman' by the neighbours who drew up his probate inventory.

The boundaries of the gentry were fluid. They were set by wealth. The sons of husbandmen and yeomen who did well could and did become gentlemen. Conversely, the younger sons of the nobility could sink into the gentry. Ancestry counted a great deal, but wealth counted for more.

The heralds were supposed to police the boundaries, by controlling the use of heraldic arms. They conducted extensive visitations of the counties in the sixteenth and seventeenth centuries, in an attempt to ensure that only those entitled to bear arms did so. The results of their labours are very useful to family historians[22]. If, however, the aim was to police the boundaries of status, they shot themselves in their feet. Many 'base and unworthy persons' could afford to pay for their arms, and some heralds were quite happy to grant them to anyone who would pay them to do so[23]. The laws of heraldry provided the only legal barrier between gentlemen and the lower orders. They were not strictly enforced, and gentility had no other legal basis. The gentry had few other legal privileges, such as the exemption from taxation they might have enjoyed in some European countries. One privilege that they did have was the right to hunt, which was denied to lesser men. But the only real obstacle preventing the lower orders becoming gentlemen was the lack of money. Gentry prejudice against the lower orders who sought to enter their ranks was strong, but ultimately could not resist wealth. The large numbers of grants of arms made in the sixteenth and seventeenth centuries suggest that admittance to the ranks of the gentry was not difficult to achieve.

The wealth of most gentry was invested in their landed estates, which had one great economic advantage as an investment: security[24]. That wealth was greatly increased by the dissolution of the monasteries, and the subsequent sell-off of monastic lands. In the early sixteenth century, more than a quarter of the acreage of England was owned by the church. It has been estimated that once the Crown had sold the estates it had seized, the gentry owned between 40% and 55% of English land[25]. Possession of it conferred power. Prior to the industrial revolution, land was the principal means of production[26]. Some gentlemen, such as the Rolles in Devon, and Sir William Petre in Essex, were able to build up substantial estates which rivalled those of the nobility. Indeed, a few, such as the Russells of Woburn and Tavistock, became peers themselves. In the century after the dissolution, many new gentry families were able to establish themselves on former monastic lands. This was reflected in the building boom of the period[27]. In Yorkshire, over 280 manor houses were either newly built or substantially altered between 1558 and 1640[28]. Many abbeys were demolished in order to make way for substantial country houses. At Lacock Abbey (Wiltshire), a new house was built on the abbey's foundations, but the cloisters were retained. Buckland Abbey (Devon) was not demolished; rather, the Drake family had it converted into a house, and lived in it. At Fountains (Yorkshire), the abbey was left to become ruinous. The new owner, Sir Stephen Proctor, used the stone from one of its domestic buildings to build himself a new house a short distance away[29].

Once, however, the government had dissipated the wealth it had acquired from dispossessed monks, the opportunities available to new gentry were much reduced. It was much harder to buy land after the mid-seventeenth century. Those who wished to emulate the Rolles or the Drakes in succeeding centuries had a more difficult task[30]. Purchase of new property for the smaller gentry was difficult. Only the profits derived from wide acres could finance that; in Yorkshire, most gentry purchasers already owned a substantial estate[31].

Large estates were the exception rather than the rule. Many men were able to consolidate their estates following the dissolution. The sitting tenants of monastic property, and those who had acted as stewards for monastic estates, were in particularly advantageous positions to benefit from the sell-off. So were the men tasked with the job of closing the monasteries down and valuing their lands.

Many gentlemen preferred to let their estates, rather than farm themselves - although they usually had a home farm, to provide for the immediate needs of their households. Minor gentry, who sometimes devoted more attention to farming than their wealthier compatriots, were the backbone of the many local and national societies which devoted their attention to encouraging more scientific agriculture. They were innovators and experimenters. They knew that commercial farming could yeild good profits, although it was a risky business. For more substantial gentry, income from rent was more secure, despite the fact that returns were lower. They too, however, did innovate: they were largely responsible for enclosing England's open fields, clearing waste land, and draining their fields. Such activities enabled them to attract the best tenants and maximise their rents[32]. Technological advances such as Rowland Vaughan's creation of water meadows in the Golden Valley, or Sir James Scudamore's breeding of new varieties of cyder apples in Herefordshire, added to their profits[33]. Even the reading of poetry could help: Thomas Tusser's poems offering *Five hundred points of good husbandry*[34] (originally published in 1573[35], and still well worth reading) provided the gentry with much good advice.

Gentry wealth was substantially increased by the opportunities presented to ambitious landlords by economic change. In the sixteenth century, both population and trade grew rapidly. The value of land went up, enabling landlords to increase their returns from rents, enclose waste land, and exploit resources such as mineral deposits and timber. Rising prices between 1760 and 1813 gave plenty of scope for enterprising gentlemen to benefit from increasing farm profits.

2. The new house at Lacock.

There could, of course, be a conflict between the need of gentlemen to increase their profits, and the moral imperative to treat their tenants well. Sir John Strode was not alone when he advised his son to 'be favourable to thy tenants'[36]. The reputation of a gentleman amongst his tenantry was important for his standing in society, and the need for fair dealing was a religious imperative.

In the seventeenth and eighteenth centuries there were also many opportunities for investment in trade and commerce. The gentry invested in shipping and colonisation, and in the exploitation of the mineral wealth which lay on their property. Fortunes were made from the extraction of coal and iron. The Glamorganshire gentry were at the forefront of industrialisation, especially between 1680 and 1710, and between 1760 and 1790. The Mansell family, for example, had substantial interests in coal and iron[37]. Many new gentry descended from urban merchant families who made their fortunes from clothing and manufacture. William Stumpe of Malmesbury succeeded in rising from being the son of a mere weaver to becoming MP for his borough, and sheriff of Wiltshire[38].

Economic factors were not all favourable to the gentry. The return they received on their investment in land was generally low, and there were long periods when rents were stagnant or falling[39]. The agricultural depression which followed the Napoleonic wars drastically reduced the incomes of those who depended on land. The financial demands of government, such as wardship in the sixteenth and early seventeenth centuries, the hearth tax in the late seventeenth century, and land tax in the eighteenth and nineteenth centuries, imposed a heavy burden on the gentry. Roman Catholic gentry in particular suffered considerably from the impositions placed upon recusants. Nevertheless, the gentry as a class managed to hang on to their landed ascendancy throughout the economic vicissitudes of the eighteenth and nineteenth centuries. They were helped by two important legal developments: the mortgage became a secure means of borrowing money, and the strict settlement provided a way to prevent heirs from alienating land from the family. In 1873, the *Return of owners of land* records the gentry as owning 55% of the land in England[40]. Between the sixteenth and the nineteenth centuries, very few major landowners suffered financial disaster to the extent that they had to sell their main seat[41].

Success, however, was not earned by the indolent. It was vital to monitor closely the business of a landed estate. Sir Nicholas Bacon's advice to his irresponsible son in law was 'to understand your own estate', and 'to take your own accompts'[42]. Thomas Tusser advised:

'Once weekelie remember thy charges to cast
Once monthlie see how thy expences may last
If quarter declareth too much to be spent
For feare of ill yeere take advise of thy rent.

Who orderlie entreth his payment in booke
May orderlie find them again (if he looke)
And he that intendeth but once for to paie
Shall find this in dooing the quietest waie'[43].

The stability of the gentry between the fifteenth and nineteenth century owed much to the emphasis placed on the nuclear family, and on the system of inheritance. Primogeniture was the rule: inheritance of the whole estate by the eldest son. The rule was, however, usually modified to make provision for younger sons, and for daughters. The aim was to preserve the main estate intact, whilst ensuring that younger sons had incomes befitting their status, and that daughters were provided with dowries.

According to Lady Mildmay, 'a private household of family (which may resemble a whole commonwealth) consist of the master and mistress, the husband and the wife, children and servants, all of one mind in love, fear and obedience, being all well chosen, instructed and governed with true judgement'[44]. The success of a gentry family depended, not just on its patriarch, but also on the relationships between all of its members. Lady Mildmay recommended obedience to the head of the family, but it was not always given. Disputes between the patriarch and his eldest son, in particular, could be disastrous. The wider kin had much less interest in the family estate, and were not normally a part of the household - but they could nevertheless have their influence, and might even inherit the estate if the direct line failed.

Landed wealth in pre-twentieth century England meant power and position. Trollope's Archdeacon Grantley was made to observe that 'Land gives so much more than the rent. It gives position and influence and political power, to say nothing about the game'[45]. The power of the gentry in the nineteenth century had changed little since the dissolution of the monasteries in the sixteenth century. That power was symbolised by the grant of honours. In the immediate aftermath of the dissolution, such grants were made very sparingly. Unlike both her predecessors, and her successors, Queen Elizabeth did not accept the idea that new wealth should be accompanied by new honours. There were 60 peers in 1500, and only 55 when she died in 1603. When James I came to the throne the floodgates of the honours system were opened. He tried to win the support of his new subjects by almost indiscriminate grants. By 1628, there were 126 peers[46], and an entirely new rank of honour: the Baronetage. James's son continued his father's policy. Faced with the threat of civil war in 1641 and 1642, Charles I granted baronetcies or knighthoods to no less than 30 members of the Yorkshire gentry, in order to win their support[47].

The Crown always needed money. James I's creation of the Baronetage initially provided a ready source of funds, although prices had to be reduced when the supply of applicants for the honour dried up. Rather less popular were the compositions imposed by Charles I on those 'of ability', that is, whose landed income was over £40 per annum, who had failed to turn up to his coronation to be knighted.

The inflation of honours[48] which the early Stuarts indulged in would have horrified Queen Elizabeth, and it was regarded as debasing the value of titles[49]. Nevertheless, it did recognise a new reality. Prior to the Reformation, the church had owned perhaps a quarter of English land. Most of that land was now in the hands of the gentry. They sought recognition of that wealth through the honours system. Their demands were reflected not only in the policies of the early Stuarts, but also in the activities of the heralds. Anyone who had a landed income of at least £10 per annum, or £300 in moveable goods, and was not 'vile born' could apply for the grant of arms. Between 1560 and 1640, the heralds made almost 4,000 grants. Nevertheless, the reputation of being a gentleman came first, a grant of arms followed[50].

Of course, not all gentry families survived. Some simply died out for lack of children. Eleven out of thirty great estates in Glamorganshire between 1721 and 1750 descended to heiresses. This in a county where the leading families in 1700 had been almost exactly the same as those in 1500[51].

Other families suffered due to the financial demands imposed by marrying off too many daughters. Well-endowed dowagers might pose severe financial problems for an estate. A substantial jointure given to a widow who lived for many years could substantially reduce the income of the head of the family. If there were two such widows in a family at the same time, the consequence could be serious financial difficulty, as Sir John Reresby of Thrybergh (Yorkshire) discovered[52]. In Northamptonshire, the Treshams were ruined by excessive hospitality and litigation[53]. Richard Goldsborough of Goldsborough (Yorkshire) spent £900 in a legal dispute; this was a major factor in the decline of his family[54]. Incompetence and extravagance spelt ruin for many. Over-indulgence in building, high-living, and political campaigning, had consequences. They were spelt out in Hardy's novel, *Tess of the d'Urberville's*. Tess's father was a nineteenth-century rural labourer who got drunk when he was told of his gentle ancestry.

Gentry could also be the victims of political or religious dissidence. In Cornwall, the Tregians were broken by their Roman Catholicism[55], and the Arundells of Helland disappeared when Sir Humphry was executed for leading the Prayer Book Rebellion in 1549, The fall of Humphrey Arundell spelt disaster for his followers. One of his retainers, Thomas Leigh, evidently played a major role in the 1549 rebellion. We have little information on what that role was; all that we know is that he was dragged off to London for trial, and narrowly escaped with his head[56].

Those families who died out were rapidly replaced by new families. Indeed, gentry economic dominance owed much to such families. It has recently been argued that the dominance of London and its merchants in the fifteenth century laid the basis of gentry wealth[57]. London's connectivity meant that the gentry congregated there. In the city, they met in Parliament, they conducted litigation, they allied themselves with its wealthy merchants, and they found marriage partners. There were few successful gentry who did not have London connections.

The gentry's success as a ruling class was largely due to the fact that it was open to those whom some of its members would have described as upstarts. There were attempts to prevent such men from joining the ranks of the landed gentry. An act of 1576 tried to stop clothiers from purchasing more than 20 acres of land[58]. It was not enforced. Hostility or not, successful merchants and lawyers could buy into the gentry and establish new county families. William Stumpe of Malmesbury was not the only Wiltshire clothier from humble origins to break into landed society. The Chivers and the Hortons also entered the ranks of the county gentry[59]. The late Princess of Wales belonged to such a family: the Spencers of Althorp owed their rise to a successful flock master[60]. Samuel Ongley, a linen draper of Cornhill, and a director of the East India Company, was able to establish his family on a landed estate in Bedfordshire[61]. Montacute House (Somerset) was built on the profits made by Sir Edward Phelips, a successful lawyer. Many gentlemen, especially if they were short of money, were prepared to marry their daughters off to wealthy citizens of London. The number of merchants who purchased country seats was small, but it was also significant[62]. According to Elton, the gentry were 'not so much a class as a form of existence, always drawing in new men and discarding failures by the wayside, frequently changing in character as circumstances changed'[63].

Another use of the term 'gentleman' must also be recognised. Service in a royal, noble, or bishop's household, or in some administrative capacity, could qualify a man to be regarded as a gentleman. Many lords had their gentlemen; so did the Crown. Such service could give men a means of entering the gentry, or at least of surviving the fact that they were younger sons without an inheritance. For some, service at court was a means to acquire wealth and the gentility which went with it. The opportunities at court steadily increased under the Tudors and Stuarts, as the royal household transformed itself into a large bureaucracy, and as the practice of appointing celibate clergyman to offices of state ceased.

It could take some time for an arriviste to be accepted in gentle society. How long, however, was a difficult question to answer. For Defoe, the question was too deep; 'it may indeed strike at the root of both the Gentry and Nobility: for all must begin somewhere, and would be traced to some less degree in their Original than will suit with the vanity of the day. It is enough therefore that we can derive for a line of two or three generations, or perhaps less'[64]. A part of the problem lay in the fact that, in some counties at least, the gentry were almost an extended family. In Kent and Cornwall, for example, most of the gentry were related to each other in some way. It would have been difficult for an outsider to break into such a society.

Most counties had several hundred 'county' families, whose members might be called upon to serve as Justices of the Peace, Members of Parliament, or Sheriffs. These offices were frequently monopolised by a small group of leading gentry. There were also many smaller 'parish gentry', who owned a few hundred acres, served in minor offices such as hundred constables and honorial stewards, and were the leading figures in their own immediate localities. Thomas Leigh, for example, who served as a retainer to Humphrey Arundel, owned a substantial farm in the remote parish of Week St. Mary, Cornwall. The Leigh family was usually listed second in the tax lists of the parish, after the entry for a junior branch of the Rolle family, who also lived there.

The gentry were the workhorses of English local government. Their ascendancy in this sphere dated from the fourteenth century, when the Crown created the office of Justice of the Peace (originally Keepers of the Peace), and invited the knights of the shires to elect Members of Parliament[65]. They staffed the bench at Quarter Sessions, they supervised the work of overseers of the poor and churchwardens, they helped to conduct musters, and to raise troops when war threatened, they organised the collection of taxes. They were the only people with the necessary time, education, and local knowledge able to undertake the essential role of acting as unpaid bureaucrats on behalf of the Crown. Those who had studied at the universities and the Inns of Court were in particularly great demand. Without the gentry, government would have been impossible. When James I noticed 'a great resort of gentlemen of quality' to London, he protested. He thought that if the provinces were deprived of their resident gentry, it would be of great prejudice to 'the generall gouverment of the kingdome', since they were the people who held all of the important government positions in the counties[66].

Most people encountered government through members of the gentry. Consequently, the gentry, to a large extent, could impose their social mores. JPs could rigorously enforce laws that suited them, such as those relating to property and game. They could, equally, neglect laws that they disliked, such as (sometimes) those which penalised their Roman Catholic gentry neighbours. The religious beliefs of the lord of the manor were the beliefs that mattered. Gentlemen could impose their religion on their local communities. In 1636, Archbishop Laud was informed that the clergy of Buckinghamshire were over-awed by puritan JPs[67]. The rise of puritanism in the late sixteenth and early seventeenth centuries was, in part, a consequence of gentry domination in local government[68]. Both puritan and Roman Catholic gentry could be viewed as classes within a class.

The expansion in gentry numbers in the sixteenth century was matched by an expansion in the number of Justices of the Peace. Sir Thomas Smith noticed that 'at first they were but four, after eight, now they come commonly to thirty or forty in every shire, either by increase of riches, learning or activity in policy or government'[69]. In Elizabethan Yorkshire, there were usually between 50 and 60 working JPs; under Charles I there were usually between 80 and 100[70]. The expansion continued in the following centuries: between 1675 and 1720, the number of JPs doubled[71]. That expansion was paralleled by the gentry take-over of borough representation in the House of Commons between the sixteenth and eighteenth centuries. It was also paralleled by a rapidly increasing workload for the Bench. William Lambarde, writing in 1582, noted that even in the fifteenth century a Lord Chief Justice had considered JPs over-burdened; in Lambarde's day, there were many more statutes. 'How many justices (thinke you), may now suffise (without breaking theyr backes) to beare so manie, not loades, but Stacks of Statutes, that have since that time bene laide uppon them'[72]. Lambarde was writing before the implementation of Poor Law legislation at the end of the sixteenth century, which added considerably to the justices' workload. Of course, most of the actual work was done by the lesser gentry, rather than the landed elite[73].

After 1873, agricultural depression brought ruin to many ancient families. Economic crisis was exacerbated by the introduction of heavy death duties in the early twentieth century. These forced the Sneyds of Keele, faced with the death of two heirs within a couple of years of each other, to sell up[74]. Like many other ancestral piles, Keele Hall has now become the centre of a major institution - Keele University. The First World War was perhaps even more devastating for gentry dominance. It decimated a whole generation of young gentlemen, the British Army's officer corps, the men who otherwise would have set the tone for British social and political life in the 1920s and 1930s. 14.9% of soldiers in their early twenties lost their lives between 1914 and 1918. Amongst Oxford graduates of the same age who served, the proportion was almost double - 27.2% lost their lives[75]. These were mostly gentlemen's sons.

Some gentle families still survive; in Devon one thinks of the Stucleys of Hartland, or the Fursdons of Fursdon. However, most gentlemen's seats have been sold off or donated to the National Trust. And most of their archives have been deposited in local record offices, where they provide invaluable resources for you, the reader of this book.

If you have gentry ancestors, you should read again the quote from William Harrison[76]. It will tell you where to look for information about your forebears. Whosoever studied the laws of the realm can be found in the registers of the Inns of Court. Whosoever studied at the universities can be found in their registers. Whosoever gave good counsel at home was probably a Justice of the Peace, or perhaps a Member of Parliament, and can be traced in the records of Quarter Sessions and central government. Captains can be traced amongst the records of the army, the militia, and the navy. The labours of the Heralds are recorded in their visitation returns, which include detailed pedigrees.

Before the nineteenth century, the only way in which men could 'live without manual labour' was to own land. Landownership was a *sine qua non* for gentlemen, who can therefore be traced by consulting deeds and other estate records. The leisure that was available to gentlemen - and their need to emphasise their lineage - also meant that they were willing and able to compile numerous family histories, pedigrees and biographies. Many of these have been published. The first step in researching gentle family histories is therefore to ask the question, 'has it been done before?'

Further Reading

The best general study of the gentry is:

- HEAL, FELICITY, & HOLMES, CLIVE. *The Gentry in England and Wales, 1500-1700.* Stanford University Press, 1994.

For a study of the elite gentry and aristocracy, see:

- STONE, LAWRENCE, & STONE, JEANNE C. FAWTIER. *An open elite? England 1540-1880.* Clarendon Press, 1984.

See also:

- MINGAY, G. E. *The Gentry: the rise and fall of a ruling class.* Longmans, 1976.

For accounts of some individual gentle families, see:

- NICOLSON, ADAM. *Gentry: six hundred years of a peculiarly English class.* Harper Press, 2012,

There are two useful works on the origins of the gentry:

- KEEN, MAURICE. *Origins of the English gentleman.* Tempus, 2002.
- COSS, PETER. *The origins of the English gentry.* Cambridge University Press, 2003.

3. Gentleman with a Cannon, 1741 by Arthur Devis (Wikimedia).

CHAPTER THREE
Has it Been Done Before?

A. Introduction

his is a question which all genealogists should ask at an early stage of their research. It is particularly important when researching gentry families. From the sixteenth century until the early twentieth century, genealogy was primarily a gentry pursuit. Quite apart from the interest in who was descended from whom, it was also a means of affirming and reinforcing status: hence the many pedigrees of the sixteenth and seventeenth centuries which purport to trace descent from Adam. Some gentry were quite happy to invent spurious ancestors in order to reinforce their status. The Pastons, for example, were actually descendants of Clement Paston, a Norfolk husbandman of the early fifteenth century. However, by 1461, his descendants had convinced themselves that they were descended from one Wulstan who came from Normandy in the eleventh century[77]. In Tudor Wales, 'the development in genealogical activity reached amazing, even frenzied, proportions'; 'families became more ostentatious owing to the attention which they gave to their heritage and their accessories, such as titles, heraldry, and armorial bearings'[78].

'Genuine genealogy', according to Stone[79], 'was cultivated by the older gentry to reassure themselves of their innate superiority over the upstarts; bogus genealogy was cultivated by the new gentry in an effort to clothe their

social nakedness'. The gentry, together with the clergy, were the only group in society with the leisure to pursue this interest.

The gentry began the study of English genealogy. Therefore, the majority of family histories and pedigrees published before the mid-twentieth century relate to gentry families. The more prominent the family, the more likely it is that it has attracted the attention of family historians.

There are innumerable published pedigrees and family histories. Unfortunately, however, there is no fully comprehensive listing. For books, it is probably best to begin by searching the catalogues of the British Library **http:/catalogue.bl.uk**, the Society of Genealogists **www.sog.org.uk/sogcat**, the Library of Congress **http:/catalog.loc.gov**, and other major research libraries. Many older family histories have been digitised. They can be found on Family History Books **http://books.familysearch.org**, Google Books **http://books.google.co.uk** and the Internet Archive **www.archive.org**. For a useful published library catalogue, see:

- MANCHESTER PUBLIC LIBRARIES. *Reference Library subject catalogue, section 929: genealogy,* ed. G. E.Haslam. 3 vols. Manchester: Libraries Committee, 1956-1958. Pt.1. is devoted to 'Pedigrees and family histories'.

Family histories in the Library of Congress are listed in:

- KAMINKOW, M. J. *Genealogies in the Library of Congress: a bibliography of family histories of America and Great Britain.* Baltimore: Magna Carta, 1974. A supplement covering accessions 1972-1976 was published in 1977. 20,000 additions held in 45 other US libraries are listed in:
- KAMINKOW, M. J. *A complement to 'Genealogies in the Library of Congress: a bibliography'.* Baltimore: Magna Carta Book Co., 1981.

These volumes only list books, not articles in journals. The latter are covered in works by Marshall (for publications pre-1903), Whitmore (1904-1950), and Barrow (1950-1975):

- MARSHALL, G. W. *The genealogist's guide.* 4th ed. Heraldry Today, 1967. Originally published 1903.
- WHITMORE, J. B. *A genealogical guide: an index to British pedigrees in continuation of Marshall's 'Genealogist's guide'.* Walford, 1953, Also published as Harleian Society vols. **99, 101, 102, & 104**. 1947-1953.
- BARROW, G. B. *The genealogist's guide: an index to printed British pedigrees and family histories, 1950-1975.* Research Publishing, 1977.

There is no general listing for publications post-1975. However, the county volumes of the present author's British genealogical bibliographies series include extensive listings of published family histories and pedigrees. Counties covered include Buckinghamshire, Cheshire, Essex, Hampshire, Lincolnshire, London and Middlesex, Norfolk, Oxfordshire, Suffolk, Surrey, Sussex, and Yorkshire. The volumes for the South-Western counties have been superseded by:

- RAYMOND, STUART A. *South West family histories: Cornwall, Devon, Dorset, Gloucestershire, Somerset, Wiltshire.* Federation of Family History Societies, 1998.

Many pedigrees appeared in genealogical journals of the nineteenth and early twentieth centuries, including the *Ancestor*, the *Collectanea topographica et genealogica*, the *Topographer & genealogist*, the *Genealogist*, and the *Miscellanea genealogica et heraldica*. These are listed in:

- RAYMOND, STUART A. *British genealogical periodicals: a bibliography of their contents.* 3 vols in 5. Federation of Family History Societies, 1991-1993. Contents: v.1. *The Ancestor; Collectanea topographica et genealogica; Topographer & Genealogist.* v.2. *The Genealogist.* v.3. *Miscellanea genealogica et heraldica.* Supplemented by *British genealogy in miscellaneous journals.* S. A. & M. J. Raymond, 1994.

More recently, many brief articles have appeared in the journals of family history societies. These were formerly regularly listed in the Federation of Family History Societies' *Federation news and digest* (1977-2006). Some societies have compiled indexes to their journals; information about these may be on their websites (listed at **www.genuki.org.uk/societies**).

Other useful listings of published family histories and pedigrees include:

- MCCOLVIN, L. R. *The librarian's subject guide to books, vol.2. Biography, family history, genealogy, etc.* James Clarke & Co., 1960. Note that this includes biographies as well as family histories.
- THOMSON, T. R. *A catalogue of British family histories.* 3rd ed. Research Publishing Co., for the Society of Genealogists, 1976.

Many web pages are devoted to the histories of particular families. These may provide valuable information, although there is no guarantee of quality. A gateway to these sites is provided by:

- Cyndis List: Surnames, Family Associations and Family Newsletters Index
  www.cyndislist.com/surnames.htm

Numerous family websites are hosted by:

- Rootsweb
  www.rootsweb.ancestry.com

B. Biographies and Biographical Dictionaries

Innumerable biographies of individual gentlemen have been published. Family historians will naturally want to read any that relate to members of their own family. Quite apart from the intrinsic interest, they are likely to include genealogical details, and a full family tree may well be found. The fact that many family histories have been digitised has already been mentioned. The same applies to biographies.

There is no comprehensive listing of biographies, but they can generally be identified in the catalogues of major research libraries. Biographies written since 1946 are listed in the annual:

- *Biography index: a cumulative index to biographical material in books and magazines.* New York: H. W. Wilson, 1946- .

For biographies published in the period 1970-1984, consult:

- *Bibliography of biography, 1970-1984.* 40 fiche + folder. British Library, 1985.

Older biographies are listed in a number of works:

- BELL, P. *Regency women: an index to biographies and memoirs.* Edinburgh: the author, 1991.
- BELL, P. *Victorian biography: a checklist of contemporary biographies of British men and women dying between 1851 and 1901.* Edinburgh: Peter Bell, 1993.
- BELL, P. *Victorian women: an index to biographies and memoirs.* Edinburgh: Peter Bell, 1989.

Biographical dictionaries provide brief biographical sketches of millions of men and women. They normally include details of parentage and families, and sometimes provide comprehensive details of where further information can be found. This certainly applies to the extensive and authoritative:

- MATHEWS, H. C. G., & HARRISON, BRIAN, eds. *Oxford dictionary of national biography.* Oxford University Press, 2004.

Entries in this dictionary can be read online **www.oxforddnb.com**. Most public libraries offer free access to this database through their own webpages. Direct subscription is expensive. No less than 57,285 biographies are included in this work. All played some prominent role in British society, and it is likely that the majority of those included would rank as gentry.

The *Oxford dictionary of national biography* is undoubtedly the most important biographical dictionary that can be found on library shelves. There are, however, many thousand more. Over 16,000 are listed in:

- SLOCUM, R. B. *Biographical dictionaries and related works: an international bibliography of more than 16,000 collective biographies, bio-bibliographies, collections of epitaphs, selected genealogical works, dictionaries of acronyms and pseudonyms, historical and specialised dictionaries, biographical material in government manuals, bibliographies of biography, biographical indexes, and selected portrait catalogs.* 2 vols. 2nd ed. Detroit: Gale Research, 1986.

Many of these dictionaries are indexed in:

- *Biography and genealogy master index: a consolidated index to more than 1,200,000 biographical sketches in over 350 current and retrospective biographical dictionaries.* Gale biographical index series **1**. 8 vols. Gale, 1980. Supplements, 1981-1985, 1986-1990, and annually from 1991. This can now be searched online at **http://search.ancestry.com/search/db.aspx?dbid=4394.**

Some 324 of the most important British biographical dictionaries are available in a microfilm collection, which is available in many large research libraries:

- *British biographical archive.* 1060 microfiche. Munich: Saur, 1984. This is also available online, at:
- World Biographical Systems Online **www.degruyter.com/cont/fb/nw/nwWbisEn.cfm**

Who's who, which has been published annually since 1849, is perhaps the best known current biographical dictionary. Entries for people who have died since 1896 have been reprinted in a series of volumes entitled *Who was who.* Entries from both of these titles are now available in an online database, which can frequently be accessed through public library websites:

- *Who's Who 2010 and Who Was Who*
  www.ukwhoswho.com

Many biographical dictionaries for particular counties were published in the early years of the twentieth century. These offer portraits and brief biographies of the late Victorian and Edwardian county gentry, plus a few aristocrats. For a full listing of these publications, consult:

- HANHAM, H. J. 'Some neglected sources of biographical information: county biographical dictionaries, 1890-1937', *Bulletin of the Institute of Historical Research*, **34**(89), 1961, pp.55-66.

For an index to most of these dictionaries, consult:

- BELL, P. *A dictionary of Edwardian biography: master index*. Edinburgh: Peter Bell, 1986.

Other biographical dictionaries specifically dealing with the gentry include:

- FOX-DAVIES, A. C. *Armorial families: a directory of gentlemen of coat armour.* 7th ed. T & E. Jack, 1929. Reprinted David & Charles 1970.
- WALFORD, EDWARD. *The county families of the United Kingdom or, Royal manual of the titled & untitled aristocracy of Great Britain & Ireland: containing a brief notice of the descent, birth, marriage, education, and appointments of each person, his heir apparent or presumptive*. Annual. Robert Hardwicke, et al, 1860-1920.
- *A directory of titled persons for the year 18—*. Whitakers, 1897-1899. Continued by *Whitaker's peerage, baronetage, knightage and companionage ...* 1900-1940. Annual companion to *Whitakers almanac*.
- *The upper ten thousand: an alphabetical list of all members of noble families, bishops, privy councillors, judges, baronets, members of the House of Commons, lords lieutenants, governors of colonies, knights and companions of orders, deans and archdeacons, and the senior officers of the army and the navy ...* George Routledge & Sons / Kelly & Co., 1875-1879. Annual; title varies. Continued by *Kelly's handbook to the titled, landed & official classes ...* Kelly & Co., 1880-1938.

Baronets fill the rank immediately below the peerage. They are the most senior members of the gentry, and are created by letters patent, which can be found on the patent rolls in The National Archives (TNA) (Class C66). Creations are announced in the *London gazette*, which can be viewed online at **www.london-gazette.co.uk.** See also:

- PARRY, C. J. *Index of Baronetage creations.* Institute of Heraldic & Genealogical Studies, 1967.

Knights created since 1665 are listed in the *London gazette* **www.london-gazette.co.uk.** For a 'complete record' of all knights, see:

- SHAW, WM. A. *The knights of England: a complete record from the earliest times to the present day of the knights of all the orders of chivalry in England, Scotland, Ireland, and of Knights Bachelors.* 2 vols. Sherratt & Hughes, 1906. Reprinted Heraldry Today, 1971.

Many biographies of medieval knights are provided in:

- MOOR, C. *Knights of Edward I.* 5 vols. Publications of the Harleian Society, **80-84.** 1929-32.

The knights of the garter are listed in:

- HOLMAN, GRACE. *The Order of the Garter: its knights and stall plates, 1348 to 1984.* 1984.

C. Obituaries

Obituaries are another important source of information. They can be found in newspapers, and in a variety of journals. Most of those published in the nineteenth century and earlier relate to members of the gentry. *The Times* took it upon itself to obituarise most public figures. Like many other newspapers, it also had a regular births, marriages and deaths column; this was used extensively by the gentry. An index to this newspaper has been published, and is available in most public libraries. It is also available online **http://archive.timesonline.co.uk/tol/archive.** Free access to this database can frequently be had through the websites of public libraries.

Many other newspapers are now being digitised for the internet, and it is becoming much easier to find obituaries and birth, marriage and death notices in them. Currently, 2,000,000 pages from 49 nineteenth-century newspapers can be searched at:

- British Newspapers 1800-1900
  http:/newspapers.bl.uk/blcs
  Free access to this website is frequently available through public library websites.

The number is likely to increase rapidly. If, however, you cannot find the information you require on this site, it may be useful to search the many other newspapers held at the British Library. For details, see:

* British Library Newspaper Reading Room
  www.bl.uk/reshelp/inrrooms/blnewspapers/newsrr.html

Most local studies libraries hold collections of newspapers for their own areas. These are listed in:

* GIBSON, JEREMY, LANGSTON, BRETT, & SMITH, BRENDA W. *Local newspapers 1750-1920, England and Wales, Channel Islands, Isle of Man: a select location list.* 3rd ed. Family History Partnership, 2011.

Obituaries are also carried in many magazines. For a collection of those published before 1800, taken from the *Gentleman's Magazine*, the *London magazine*, the *European Magazine,* and others, consult:

* MUSGRAVE, W. *Obituary prior to 1800 (as far as it relates to England, Scotland and Ireland).* 6 vols. Harleian Society, **44-9**. 1899-1901.

Many obituary notices are indexed in:

* 'Index of obituary notices for the year 1878', in *Report of the first annual meeting of the Index Society.* Index Society publications **4**. 1878, pp.97-121. Continued for 1880 in the 2nd Report, and for 1880-1882 as full volumes of the Society's publications, **9, 12, & 14**.

The *Gentleman's Magazine* was published between 1731 and 1907, and included many obituaries, especially prior to 1868. Some are included in Musgrave's *Obituaries,* as already noted. The value of this magazine for genealogists is discussed in:

* CHRISTIE, P. 'The *Gentleman's Magazine* as a source for the family historian', *Genealogists' Magazine* **20**, 1981, pp.238-239.

See also:

* Wikipedia: The *Gentleman's Magazine*
  http://en.wikipedia.org/wiki/The_Gentleman's_Magazine

The Gentleman's *Magazine :*

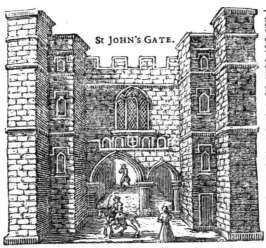

St John's Gate.

Lond Gazette
Londo Jour.
Fog's Journ.
Applebee's ::
Read's :: : :
Craftsman ::
D. Spectator
Grubstreet I
W.ly Register
Free = Briton
Hyp = Doctor
Daily Court.
Daily = Post
Dai.___ournal
Da. Post-boy
D. Advertiser
EveningPost
St James's Eb.
Whitehall Eb.
Lodon Eveig
___lying = Post
Weekly Mis-
cellany.

York 2 News
Dublin 6 :::
Edinburgh 2
Bristol :: : ::
Norwich 2 ::
Exeter 2 :
Worcester
Northampton
Gloucester
Stamford : :
Nottingham
Bury Journ.
Chester ditto
Derby ditto
Ipswich dit.
Reading dit.
Leeds Merc.
Newcastle C.
Canterbury
Manchester :
Boston :::
Jamaica, &c
Barbados :

Or, MONTHLY INTELLIGENCER.

For JANUARY, 1731.

CONTAINING,

/more in Quantity, and greater Variety, than any Book of the Kind and Price./

I. A VIEW of the WEEKLY ESSAYS, *viz.* Of Queen *Elizabeth* ; Ministers ; Treaties ; Liberty of the Press ; Riot Act ; Armies ; Traytors ; Patriots ; Reason ; Criticism ; Versifying ; Ridicule ; Humours ; Love ; Prostitutes ; Musick ; Pawn-brokers ; Surgery ; Law.
II. POETRY. The Ode for the New Year, by *Colly Cibber*, Esq; Remarks upon it ; Imitations of it, by way of *Burlesque* ; Verses on the same Subject ; ingenious Epitaphs and Epigrams.
III. DOMESTICK OCCURRENCES ; *viz.* Births, Deaths, Marriages, Preferments,

Casualties, Burials and Christenings in London.
IV. Melancholy Effects of Credulity in *Witchcraft*.
V. Prices of Goods, Grain, Stocks, and a List of Bankrupts.
VI. A correct List of the Sheriffs for the current Year.
VII. Remarkable Advertisements.
VIII. FOREIGN Affairs, with an Introduction to this Year's History.
IX. REGISTER of Books.
X. Observations on Gardening.
XI. Table of CONTENTS.

By *SYLVANUS URBAN*, Gent.

The FIFTH EDITION.

LONDON : Printed for the AUTHOR, and sold at St *John's Gate :* By F. *Jefferies*, in *Ludgate-street* ; all other Booksellers ; and by the Persons who serve Gentlemen with the News-papers : *Of whom may be had* Compleat Sets, *or any* single Number.

A few are printed on ROYAL PAPER, *large Margin,* for the CURIOUS.

4. *The Gentleman's Magazine (Wikimedia).*

Two indexes to early obituaries in this magazine are available:

- FARRAR, R. H. *An index to the biographical and obituary notices in the Gentleman's Magazine, 1731-80.* Index Library, **15**. British Record Society, 1891.
- NANGLE, B. *The Gentleman's Magazine biographical and obituary notices, 1781-1819: an index.* Garland reference library of the Humanities, 212. New York: Garland, 1980.

Early issues of the *Gentleman's Magazine* (1731-1750) have been digitised, and can be searched at:

- Internet Library of Early Journal
  www.bodley.ox.ac.uk/ilej/
  This database also includes digitised images of a number of other eighteenth-century journals, some of which may include obituaries. It should be noted that the **Ancestry.com** database, *The Gentleman's Magazine Library, 1731-1868*, only contains abstracts from the original magazine, and does not include most obituaries.

Birth, marriage and death notices in newspapers and magazines have rarely been separately indexed. However, a single year is covered in:

- LOCKE, A. *Locke's annual register of births, marriages and deaths, 1891.* Charles Dickens & Evans, 1891.

For those who died in the early nineteenth century, it may be useful to consult:

- *The annual biography and obituary ...* Longman, Hurst, Rees, Orme & Brown, 1817-1837.

D. Pedigrees and Pedigree Collections

Much of the effort of early genealogists and antiquaries focused on the compilation of pedigrees. The visitation pedigrees compiled by Heralds are particularly important, and will be discussed in section E below. Many unpublished pedigrees can be found amongst collections of family papers held by both local and national record offices. There are several union catalogues which will help you to identify these:

- A2A: Access to Archives
  www.nationalarchives.gov.uk/a2a
  Indexes the holdings of over 400 record offices

- Archives Hub
  www.archiveshub.ac.uk
  Union catalogue for university and college archives

- Aim 25: Archives in London and the M25 Area
  www.aim25.ac.uk

It is important to appreciate that none of these list everything held by participating institutions. A2A, for example, estimates that only 30% of UK archives are listed. It is always worth checking with individual record offices to see whether they hold any unlisted material.

Many manuscript pedigrees are held in the British Library. These are listed at:

- British Library Manuscripts Catalogue
  www.bl.uk/catalogues/manuscripts/INDEX.asp

An index to the British Library's manuscripts is also available in print:

- *Index of manuscripts in the British Library*. 10 vols. Chadwyck-Healey, 1984-1986.

An extensive collection of pedigrees is held by the Society of Genealogists. These are listed at:

- Society of Genealogists: Index to the Pedigree Collection
  www.sog.org.uk/library/pedigree.shtml

Numerous pedigrees of the gentry were included in the many county and local histories published in the nineteenth century and earlier. Many of these are indexed by Marshall (see above, p.20). See also:

- BRIDGER, C. *An index to printed pedigrees, contained in county and local histories, the heralds' visitations, and in more important genealogical collections.* J. R. Smith, 1867. Reprinted Baltimore: Genealogical Publishing Co., 1969.
- COLEMAN, J. *Coleman's general index to printed pedigrees which are to be found in all principal county and local histories, and in many privately printed genealogies.* The author, 1866.

There are a number of major collections of published pedigrees, which deal specifically with the landed classes. The gentry and the peerage were frequently closely related. Some collections deal with the peerage or the gentry; others cover both. They cannot be entirely separated; those which are solely devoted to the peerage and baronetage also incidentally include much information on younger sons who joined the gentry, and on brides who held a lower rank in society - but perhaps greater wealth.

Pedigrees of royalty are also worth consulting. Many gentry (and others) could claim royal connections. For an introduction to royal lineages, consult:

• *Burke's guide to the royal family.* Burke's Peerage, 1973.

More detailed works, essential for establishing a royal descent (although incomplete), include:

• RUVIGNY & RAINEVILLE, MARQUIS OF. *The blood royal of Britain : being a roll of the living descendants of Edward IV and Henry VII, Kings of England, and James III, King of Scotland.* T. C. & E. C. Jack, 1903.
• RUVIGNY & RAINEVILLE, MARQUIS OF. *The Plantagenet roll of the blood royal, being a complete table of all the descendants of Edward III, king of England.* 4 vols. T. C. & E. Jack, 1907-1911.

The pedigrees of 200 families who claimed royal descent are printed in:

• BURKE, BERNARD. *The royal families of England, Scotland, and Wales: with pedigrees of royal descents in illustration.* Harrison, 1876.

The authoritative work on the peerage is:

• COKAYNE, G.E. *The complete Peerage of England, Scotland, Ireland, Great Britain and the United Kingdom, extant or dormant.* New ed. 13 vols. in 6. Sutton, 1981. Originally published St. Catherine's Press, 1910-1959.

For a discussion of the importance of this work, consult:

• HAMMOND, P. 'The Complete peerage', *Genealogists' Magazine* **24**(11), 1994, pp.495-499.

Brief details of peerages, giving dates and family names, can be found in:

• LEESON, FRANCIS L. *A directory of British peerages, from the earliest times to the present day.* Rev. ed. Society of Genealogists Enterprises, 2002.

See also:

- COLLINS, ARTHUR. *Collins Peerage of England*, ed. Sir Egerton Brydges. 9 vols. F. C. & J. Rivington, 1812.

For the extinct Peerage, consult:

- PINE, L. G. *The new extinct peerage, 1884-1971: containing extinct, abeyant, dormant, and suspended peerages with genealogies and arms.* Heraldry Today, 1972.

For baronets' pedigrees, consult:

- C[OKAYNE], G. E. *The complete baronetage.* Microprint ed. 6 vols. in 1. Sutton, 1983. Originally published 1900-1909.

Many pedigree collections cover the Peerage, the Baronetage, and the landed gentry together. Burke's were probably the most prolific publishers in this field. They have published over 100 editions of titles such as *Burke's landed gentry*, and *Burke's peerage, baronetage and knightage.* It has been calculated that over 90% of landed gentry families are included in the 15th, 17th and 18th editions of:

- BURKE, J., & BURKE, B. *A genealogical and heraldic history of the landed gentry,* ed. P. Townend. 18th ed. 2 vols. Burke's Peerage, 1965.

For an essay on the scope of this compilation, see:

- SAYER, M. J. 'The scope of Burke's landed gentry', *Genealogists' Magazine* **19**, 1977, pp.120-124.

Most reference libraries hold copies of some Burke titles, all of which are comprehensively indexed in:

- *Burke's family index.* Burke's Peerage, 1976.

Many Burke publications can now be searched online:

- Burke's Peerage and Gentry
  www.burkespeerage.com

Another well-known publication, which is less comprehensive than Burke's, but includes more information on contemporary family members, is:

- *Debrett's peerage, baronetage and knightage and companionage.* Dean & Son, et al, 1784- . There are numerous editions of this work, although recent editions only cover the peerage and baronetage.

See also:

- *Dod's peerage. baronetage and knightage of Great Britain and Ireland.* Gilbert & Rivington, 1904- .

For the knightage, consult:

- MARSHALL, G.W., ed. *Le Neve's pedigrees of the knights made by King Charles II, King James II, King William III, and Queen Mary, King William alone, and Queen Anne.* Publications of the Harleian Society 8. 1873.

One of the largest published collections of pedigrees (not to be confused with heraldic visitations) is:

- HOWARD, J. J., & CRISP, F. A. *Visitation of England and Wales.* 21 vols + 14 vols of 'notes'. Privately printed, 1893-1921. This is indexed in:
- WILLIAMSON, W. W. 'An index to the pedigrees in Howard & Crisp's Visitation of England and Wales', *Norfolk ancestor* 1(4), 1978, pp.46-50.

Other general collections of pedigrees include:

- *Pedigree register.* 3 vols. George Sherwood, 1907-1916.
- GWYNN-JONES, P. LLOYD, & TOVEY, SUSANNA. *The Bigland pedigree index: an index to the pedigrees in the genealogical manuscripts of Sir Ralph Bigland, Garter King of Arms, from a manuscript index in the College of Arms.* Harleian Society, New series **9**. 1990.

Some medieval pedigrees are printed in:

- WROTTESLEY, G. *Pedigrees from the plea rolls, collected from the pleadings in the various courts of law, A.D. 1200 to 1500.* Harrison & Son, [1905].

Pedigrees of the lesser gentry, especially in the North of England, can be found in:

- HUNTER, J. *Familiae minorum gentium*, ed. J. W. Clay. Harleian Society, **37-40**. 1894-6.
- HUNTER, J. *Hunter's pedigrees: a continuation of 'Familiae minorum gentium diligentia Josephi Hunter, Sheffieldiensis'*, ed. J. W. Walker. Harleian Society visitations, **88**. 1936.

There are also numerous collections of pedigrees relating to particular counties, too many to list here. They can be identified in the county bibliographies of the present author, which have already been mentioned.

E. Heraldic Visitations

The collections of pedigrees compiled by the heralds on their visitations of the counties, and now (mostly) held by the College of Arms, form perhaps the most substantial collections of pedigrees from the Tudor and Stuart eras now in existence. The end of continuous war in the mid-fifteenth century reduced the diplomatic need for heralds to act as messengers, and gave them more time to concentrate on heraldic and genealogical activities. The Crown was keen to control the proliferation of arms, and founded the College in 1484 in order to provide a degree of regulation. The heralds began to conduct county visitations in the late fifteenth century[80], although extensive evidence for their visitation activities is not available before 1530. Heraldic visitations continued until 1688, with major series of visitations conducted c.1580, 1620, and 1666.

The heralds began their work by obtaining a commission from the Crown, and asking the sheriff of each county to compile a list of all the local nobles, knights, and gentlemen who bore arms. This might be based on tax lists, freeholders returns, and similar lists, and informed by the local knowledge of high constables and other officers. The aim was to identify all those who, on the basis of their wealth and status, might be regarded as armigerous by local people[81]. These lists were used by the heralds to determine who was to be summoned to attend their visitations. Sometimes these lists survive. Not everyone who was summoned actually claimed armigerous status. Some were quite content to disclaim any right to arms. Their signed disclaimers were proclaimed at Assizes. The fact that some of those who were summoned were not armigerous may, however, have given rise to suspicions. Sometimes, leading gentry took a dim view of the heralds' proceedings. William Harbin, for example, thought that the aim of the visitation was actually 'more to grant new coats of arms to new upstart families than to review the ancient gentlemen's coats'. He claimed that 'neither any of the ancients appeared at all in our county'[82]. In London, some 50% of those summoned failed to appear[83], but probably for a different reason. Wealthy tradesmen were not always interested in entering the ranks of the gentry.

Harbin was rather hard on the heralds. It is true that they were happy to grant coats of arms to anyone who could afford them. It is also true that the demand for coat armour was rapidly increasing; over 2000 grants of arms were made between 1560 and 1589 - far more than in any earlier period of 30 years[84]. However, Squibb argues that 'it is somewhat remarkable that in an age when the officers of arms were prepared to provide their private clients with pedigrees of inordinate length and incredible splendour, they should have displayed such rectitude when engaged in their official duties on behalf of the Crown'[85].

Proof of the right to bear arms could be provided by the personal knowledge of heads of families, traditions that had been handed down in the family, and family muniments such as charters, seals, or letters patent granting arms. Heraldic insignia and inscriptions on tombs, and in stained glass windows, was also important. Many monuments, and much stained glass, was destroyed during the Reformation and the Civil War: occasionally the evidence they contained had been recorded by the heralds, or perhaps by other antiquaries[86].

Heralds began by recording the evidence provided, and then compiled pedigrees based on that evidence. A typical entry in the 1687 visitation of London begins by indicating the place where the family currently resided, and blazons their arms. It then gives details of the family's descent through eldest sons for several generations, noting ages and origins. For example, we learn that William Smith, the beadle of Cornhill Ward, was aged 79, and that his grandfather John Smith came from Church Lawford (Warwickshire)[87].

These visitation pedigrees contain much information that would otherwise have been lost. They are not, however, perfect. They contain as much or as little information as the families concerned wanted the heralds to know. Sometimes, that was very little - just enough to ensure that the right to arms was recognised. Others gave false information. Anyone who claimed arms or a title but could not prove their right was required to acknowledge, in writing, 'that we do not know of any arms belonging to us nor do we make claim to arms or gentility'. The most comprehensive published list of disclaimers is:

- RYLANDS, J. P. *Disclaimers at the Heralds visitations*. 1888[88].

Visitation pedigrees are one of the few original sources that were specifically compiled for genealogical purposes. Like other sources, they require careful evaluation. That is particularly important in light of the fact that most genealogists are likely to use printed editions, rather than the originals in the College of Arms. Unfortunately, the collections of the College are not available to the general public. Reliance must therefore be placed on the numerous copies held in the British Library and other repositories, and on the many published editions.

The Harleian Society **http://fmg.ac/Harleian/Society.htm** has devoted most of its attention to publishing heraldic visitation returns; its publications are listed on its website. A number of local record societies have also published them.

Unfortunately, the quality of published visitations is very variable. Indeed, some collections of pedigrees described as visitations actually have nothing to do with the heralds. Reference has already been made to Howard & Crisp's *Visitation of England and Wales*. Useful as it may be, it was not compiled by heralds at their visitations. The same can be said of the so-called *Visitation of Bedfordshire*, published as volume 19 of the Harleian Society's series. Its pedigrees were not compiled by the heralds, despite its title. Many are by persons unknown. Other early editions of visitations share similar faults.

Many published editions of visitations are taken from copies in the British Library, rather than from the originals in the College of Arms. Some of these so-called 'copies' are in fact conflations of several successive visitations, sometimes also including material from other sources as well. The quality of the work of editors must also sometimes be called into question. Even the best editions may contain copyists' errors and typesetters' mis-prints[89]. This is doubly unfortunate in light of the fact that the original manuscripts cannot be consulted by most of us. It is always important to the genealogist to discover the source of the information that is being used.

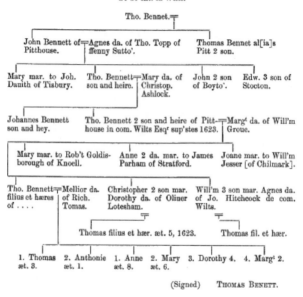

Bennett.

[Harl. 1166, fo. 34ᵇ.]

ARMS.—*Quarterly*—1 and 4, [*Per pale argent and or,*] *an eagle displayed with two heads gules ; 2 and 3, Sable, a chevron ermine between three Katherine-wheels argent.*
CREST.—*A chough sable, beaked and legged gules, standing on a whelkshell or.*

To be ent. in Wilts.

Tho. Bennet.⊤

John Bennett of⊤Agnes da. of Tho. Topp of   Thomas Bennet al[ia]s
Pitthouse.   │ffenny Sutto'.   Pitt 2 son.

Mary mar. to Joh.   Tho. Bennett⊤Mary da. of   John 2 son   Edw. 3 son of
Danith of Tisbury. son and heire.│Christop.   of Boyto'.   Stocton.
                                   │Ashlock.

Johannes Bennett   Tho. Bennett 2 son and heire of Pitt-⊤Margᵗ da. of Will'm
son and hey.   house in com. Wilts Esqʳ sup'stes 1623.│Groue.

Mary mar. to Rob't Goldis-   Anne 2 da. mar. to James   Joane mar. to Will'm
borough of Knoell.   Parham of Stratford.   Jesser [of Chilmark].

Tho. Bennett⊤Mellior da.   Christopher 2 son mar.   Will'm 3 son mar. Agnes da.
filius et hæres│of Rich.   Dorothy da. of Oliuer   of Jo. Hitchcock de com.
of . . . .   │Tomas.   Lotesham.   Wilts.
                                            ⊤   ⊤
            Thomas filius et hær. æt. 5, 1623.   Thomas fil. et hær.

1. Thomas   2. Anthonie   1. Anne   2. Mary   3. Dorothy 4.   4. Margᵗ 2.
æt. 3.   æt. 1.   æt. 8.   æt. 6.

(Signed)   THOMAS BENETT.

5. *Pedigree of Bennett, taken from* JOHN PAUL RYLANDS, *ed. The visitation of Dorset taken in the year 1623 ... Publications of the Harleian Society, 20. 1885.*

Despite these caveats, the printed visitation pedigrees can be very useful, and are sometimes indispensable. Some, indeed, are fine examples of the editors' art. One recent edition from the Harleian Society is not only based primarily on the official original record of the visitation held in the College of Arms, it also has a detailed introduction which is worth reading by everyone who needs to consult visitations. There are also transcripts of returns by the beadles, listing the gentlemen who lived in their wards, abstracts from the working notebooks used during the visitation (one of which is in the Guildhall Library), and details of disclaimers. These documents are typical of those created at other visitations. See:

• WALES, T. C., & HARTLEY, C. P., eds. *The visitation of London begun in 1687.* 2 vols. Publications of the Harleian Society, new series **16-17**. 2004.

Many individual pedigrees taken directly from the original manuscripts in the College of Arms were published in the nineteenth and early twentieth centuries, in journals such as the *Genealogist* and *Miscellanea genealogica et heraldica*. These can sometimes be used to check the accuracy of the returns published by the Harleian Society, and are available in many major reference libraries[90].

Visitation pedigrees published by the Harleian Society, in genealogical journals, and elsewhere, are all listed in the works by Marshall, Whitmore, and Barrow listed above, p.20. Comprehensive lists of published visitation returns, copies, and the original manuscripts are provided by:

- HUMPHERY-SMITH, C. R. *Armigerous ancestors and those who weren't: a catalogue of visitation records, together with an index of pedigrees, arms, and disclaimers*. Institute of Heraldic & Genealogical Studies, 1997.
- PHILLIPPS, SIR THOMAS. *Herald's visitation index: a collection of disclaimers from several sources*. 1854. This is reproduced in *Armigerous ancestors* (see above). A zincographed version of this work, entitled *Herald's visitation disclaimers*, is digitised at **http://dbooks.bodleian.ox.ac.uk/books/PDFs/555094546.pdf**
- SIMS, R. *An index to the pedigrees contained in the Heralds' visitations and other manuscripts in the British Museum*. J. R. Smith, 1849. Reprinted Baltimore: Genealogical Publishing, 1970. This is also reproduced in *Armigerous ancestors* (see above)

For an earlier listing, see:

- NICHOLAS, N. H. *Catalogue of the heralds visitations, with references to many other valuable genealogical and topographical manuscripts in the British Museum*. 2nd ed. Taylor, 1825.

For the records of the College of Arms, consult:

- CAMPBELL, LOUISE, & STEER, FRANCIS. *A catalogue of manuscripts in the College of Arms collections. Volume 1*. College of Arms, 1988.

Useful information on the College can be found on its website:

- College of Arms
  www.college-of-arms.gov.uk

ST GEORGE.

St George = Mary Lucas. of Burtenham.

33. TALBOYS E.I.N.

[Quartered with Welles]

Anne sister of Gilbert = Sir Edw. Dymoke
Lord Talboys of Kyme   of Scrivelsby Champion
p. 10. 50.   at coronation of Ed. VI.
                       Mary & Elizabeth.

25. YESCI V.E. 1210.

...... Lucas. 40.

Israel = William de Welles
de Vesci   p. 55. 57.

GE.

gettle = Edward Ridge
of Besham Park.
In Worcester.
p. 51.

37. WILLOUGHBY.

of Parham.

Cicely de Welles = Robt. Lord Willoughby.
Heires of the Barony
of Welles 3 p 55. 56. 56c.

Richard Welles = Joane dau. g Lord
Willoughby D'Eesby.
p. 55.

38. BIRD

William James = Agnes Bird.
Lucas. of Witham.   p. 6. 19. 72.

E. Earls of Hardwick.
= Philip Yorke
Earl of Hardwick.
p. 7. 15. 16. 16.9

42. AN...

FRANKLYN
of Wye

Asher Franklyn = of Wye
married   dau. of Rob.
Lucas. Esq. of Wandsworth.

6. Illuminated manuscript form the SoG special collections.

CHAPTER FOUR
Heraldry

The gentry, together with the aristocracy, were obsessed by rank and precedence. Their landed property enabled them to secure grants of honours from the Crown. These honours were symbolised by heraldry, which enabled them to display their rank and power. Heraldic insignia were 'a visual expression of status within the public sphere'[91]. The possession of heraldic arms denoted a sure place in the ranks of gentry society. Arms were granted to specific individuals and their heirs. Contrary to popular belief, they cannot be claimed simply because the claimant bears the same surname. It is extremely unlikely that anyone entitled to bear arms has no knowledge of that entitlement.

All members of the gentry were armorial, that is, they had the right to bear arms, or at least to apply for them. As the gentry increased in number, and became more differentiated from each other, so the rules of heraldry became increasingly complex and intricate. Many books have been written on the subject; it is not possible to do more here than offer a brief summary, and make some suggestions for further study.

Heraldry can be found in many different places - on the walls of old houses, in books and on book plates, on clothing and armour, on medals. Perhaps the commonest place for family historians to find heraldic evidence is on tombstones and memorials in churches and churchyards. In many instances,

churches were built close beside the houses of manorial lords, and are full of memorials to those lords. Indeed, some are more like mausoleums than parish churches. For example, the church of St Mary at Lydiard Tregoze (Wiltshire) is full of memorials to the St John family[92]. The more substantial memorials loudly proclaim that the individuals they memorialise were leading figures in their communities, happy to make a public display of their position in society. They are intended to reflect well on their subjects, and for that reason deserve critical scrutiny from researchers.

Many transcripts of memorial inscriptions have been made by family history societies and others. Recent transcriptions are not likely to focus on the gentry. However, transcripts made in the nineteenth century and earlier are likely to do so[93]. For an example, see:

- SHERLOCK, PETER, ed. *Monumental inscriptions of Wiltshire.* Wiltshire Record Society, 53. 2000.

Memorials come in various different shapes and sizes. Those in churches developed from the carving of designs on coffin lids and stone slabs inset into floors. These incised slabs rarely had heraldic devices, apart perhaps from small shields. Many have suffered from excessive wear, or been lost. Sometimes they have been lifted from the floor and set upright against walls.

In the seventeenth century, ledger stones replaced incised slabs. They did not depict the deceased, but bore simple inscriptions, and deeply incised roundels with heraldic devices. They were frequently set in the floor above interments, or formed part of tomb chests.

The effigy was a more noticeable memorial. The late thirteenth and early fourteenth centuries witnessed 'a virtual colonisation of England's churches by the knightly effigy'[94]. These were stylistic representations of bodies, rather than taken from life. They provide substantial evidence for the development of costume and armour during the medieval period. Early knights' effigies usually bear heraldic shields, which were carved and painted. The paint has usually disappeared, but if there is no inscription the arms may provide the only means of identifying the person memorialised. From the mid-fourteenth century, heraldic representations are more likely to be carved on tomb chests or canopies, rather than on the effigy itself.

Monumental brasses provided a cheaper means of memorialising their subjects. The brass was an alloy of copper, zinc, and other metals, sometimes known as latten. Figures, sometimes life sized, were engraved on the metal, which was fixed into indentations carved from a stone slab, so that the surface was flush. These figures were surrounded by inscriptions, frequently in Latin, together with heraldic devices.

These memorials were not necessarily contemporaneous with the death of their subjects. Some were commissioned long before the death took place. Others were created many years later. Nor do they necessarily mark the place of interment, although ledger stones are more likely to do so. Crusaders, for example, who died in battle, were frequently buried in the East, but memorialized at home. Sometimes hearts were buried separately from the body.

In the sixteenth century, effigies began to be more substantial in size. Sometimes memorials included a whole family, with husband and wife lying together, surrounded by their kneeling children. The memorial to the Savage family at Elmley Castle (Worcestershire) depicts four sons kneeling at the feet of their parents, whilst Lady Catherine cradles her 'darling little daughter' in her arms[95].

7. Wall memorial in Topsham (Devon) Church.

Wall memorials became common in the late sixteenth and seventeenth centuries; they frequently depicted heads, had wordier inscriptions (sometimes in Latin), and included a proliferation of heraldic devices. In the eighteenth and nineteenth centuries, the use of heraldry in wall memorials declined, but the same period saw an increasing use of hatchments.

8. The Hatchment of Ellen, wife of Sir Bourchier Wrey, Bt., at Tawstock (Devon).

Hatchments are depictions of heraldic arms and other insignia painted on lozenge-shaped boards or canvas. They were intended to be hung outside the house of the deceased during the mourning period, and were subsequently removed to be hung in their parish church. For a detailed catalogue of hatchments, consult:

• SUMMERS, PETER, et al. *Hatchments in Britain*. 10 vols. Phillimore, 1974-1994.

The heraldry depicted on memorials and elsewhere is governed by strict rules, although a particular achievement can be painted in a variety of different ways. It is based upon a written description or blazon. It is the blazon, not the actual design, which is the legal property of the bearer. It is therefore necessary to understand the technical terms used in blazoning. They give the tincture - that is, the colour - of the shield, describe the various ways in which shields are partitioned, and identify the various animals and objects which are used as charges - that is, pictorial representations. A brief example of a blazon (for the Bourchier Wrey hatchment) is given below.

The achievement is the complete representation of an individual's heraldic insignia. It may include crests, supporters, helmets, mottoes, badges, helms, etc., as well as the actual coat of arms. Sometimes the term 'coat of arms' is used to denote the whole achievement. Technically, this is not correct; it should be reserved for the shield alone.

Each achievement is unique to its bearer. Marks of cadency are used to preserve that uniqueness when arms descend to heirs. These distinguish the arms of the eldest son from those of his brothers. It is therefore possible to identify which brother bore particular arms.

Heraldry can also be used to denote marriage alliances. A husband is entitled to impale his father-in-law's arms on his own shield, that is, he can place his own arms on the left of the shield, and his wife's family arms on the right. If his wife is an heiress, without brothers, her arms can be placed on a small shield which covers the centre of his own shield. The children of an heiress may quarter their shields, placing paternal arms in the first and fourth quarters, maternal arms in the second and third. In the next generation, these quartered coats may be quartered again, ad infinitum. Impalement can also be used by office holders, such as bishops, to link their official positions with their own personal arms.

The hatchment in illustration 8 is that of Sir Bourchier Wrey, 6th Baronet, who died in 1784. It shows the red hand of Ulster, indicating that he was a baronet, and quarters Wrey, Bourchier, Woodstock, and Bohun. Bourchier married Ellen, the daughter of John Thresher. Her arms are on an escutcheon of pretence, which indicates that she was an heiress or co-heiress, and that any future generations would also quarter her coat. In fact, there were no surviving offspring; that is shown by the skull in base. The dexter background is black, and the sinister white, indicating that the husband had died and the wife survived. The helmet is that of a knight or gentleman, although it should have been a baronet's helmet, which faces straight forward. The Wrey quartering is blazoned as 'sable, a fess between three pole-axes helved gules'. 'Sable' indicates a black background, 'fess' is the bar separating the top and bottom of the shield, the 'helves' are the handles of the axes, which are guled, or coloured red[96]. The texts listed below includes a number of works which will help you to understand the language of blazoning.

If one of your ancestors did bear a coat of arms, it may be that you could use it to trace their medieval descent. The authoritative listing is now:

* CHESSHYRE, D. H. B., & WOODCOCK, T., et al. *Dictionary of British arms: medieval ordinary.* 4 vols. Society of Antiquaries, 1992- . Vols 1-3 so far published.

For blazons of arms by surname, see also:

* BURKE, SIR BERNARD. *The general armory of England, Scotland, Ireland and Wales, comprising a register of armorial bearings from the earliest to the present time.* Harrison, 1884. This is supplemented by:
* HUMPHERY-SMITH, CECIL R., *ed. General armory two: Alfred Morant's additions and corrections to Burke's general armory.* Tabard Press, 1973.

Crests are listed in:

* FAIRBAIRN, JAMES. *Fairbairn's crests of the families of Great Britain and Ireland,* revised by Laurence Butters. New Orchard, 1986.

These are, of course, modern compilations. They are largely based on rolls of arms, and on grants of arms. Original manuscript rolls, together with some published editions, are listed by:

* WAGNER, ANTHONY RICHARD. *A catalogue of English medieval rolls of arms.* Society of Antiquraries, 1948. Also published by the Harleian Society. This is supplemented by:
* TREMLETT, THOMAS DANIEL, ed. *Rolls of arms, Henry III.* Society of Antiquaries, 1967.

Grants of arms are also important. Many collections of grants are held by the British Library, and may be found through its manuscript catalogue **www.bl.uk/ catalogue/manuscripts**. These, together with a number of other collections, are indexed in:

* RYLANDS, W. HARRY, ed. *Grantees of arms named in docquets and patents to the end of the seventeenth century, in the manuscripts preserved in the British Museum, the Bodleian Library, Oxford, Queen s College, Oxford, Gonville and Caius College, Cambridge, and elsewhere, alphabetically arranged by the late Joseph Foster, and contained in the Additional ms no 37,147 in the British Museum.* Publications of the Harleian Society **66**. 1915.

- RYLANDS, W. HARRY, ed. *Grantees of arms named in docquets and patents between the years 1687 and 1898, preserved in various manuscripts collected and arranged by the late Joseph Foster, and contained in the Additional ms no 37,149 in the British Museum.* 2 vols. Publications of the Harleian Society 67-8. 1916-1917.

Much useful information is provided by the funeral certificates which heralds were supposed to deposit in the College of Arms whenever they served at a funeral. These provide information regarding the time of death, the place of burial and details of the marriages, issue, and frequently details of other family members, as well as the names of those attending[97]. Most of these certificates are still held by the College of Arms, which is unfortunately not open for personal research. A few, however, are in TNA, class SP17. These mainly relate to Derbyshire, Nottinghamshire, and Wales. For some published funeral certificates, see:

- RYLANDS, JOHN PAUL, ed. *Cheshire and Lancashire funeral certificates, AD 1600 to 1678.* Lancashire & Cheshire Record Society, **6**.1882.
- KING, THOMAS WILLIAM, ed. *Lancashire funeral certificates.* Chetham Society old series 75. 1869.

Miscellaneous heraldic documents can be consulted in:

- LITTLEDALE, WILLOUGHBY A., ed. *A collection of miscellaneous grants, crests, confirmations, augmentations and exemplifications of arms in the MSS. preserved in the British Museum, Ashmolean Library, Queen's College, Oxford, and elsewhere.* Harleian Society **76-77**. 1925-1926.

It is much more difficult to identify families from particular coats of arms. If its date and geographical origin can be identified, that would be useful information. The coat of arms must be blazoned, that is, verbally described according to the rules of heraldry. That description must then be used to search an ordinary, that is, a book which lists arms by their features rather than by name. Unfortunately, there is no complete ordinary of English arms. The best is:

- PAPWORTH, JOHN WOODY. *Ordinary of British Armorials: An Alphabetical Dictionary of Coats of Arms Belonging to Families in Great Britain & Ireland.* London: T. Richards, 1874. (various reprints).

Ordinaries are also included in many medieval rolls of arms, many of which are listed by Wagner (see above, p.44.)

Further Reading

- BROOKE-LITTLE, J. P. *Boutell's heraldry.* Rev ed. Frederick Warne, 1978.
- FOX-DAVIES, ARTHUR CHARLES. *A complete guide to heraldry.* T. C. & E. C. Jack, 1929. Reprinted Bracken Books, 1993.
- FRIAR, STEPHEN. *The Sutton companion to heraldry.* New ed. Sutton Publishing, 2004.
- WOODCOCK, THOMAS, & ROBINSON, JOHN MARTIN. *The Oxford guide to heraldry.* Oxford University Press, 1988.

A useful dictionary is provided by:

- FRIAR, STEPHEN. *A new dictionary of heraldry.* A. & C. Black, 1987.

There are a substantial number of works dealing with monumental brasses, which cannot all be listed here. A useful bibliography is included on the website of:

- The Monumental Brass Society
  www.mbs-brasses.co.uk

Comprehensive listings of brasses are currently being published in this Society's county series. Details are on its website. For the counties not covered so far, it may be useful to consult:

- STEPHENSON, MILL. *A list of monumental brasses in the British Isles.* Headley Brothers, 1926. This is supplemented by:
- GRIFFIN, R. *Appendix to a list of monumental brasses in the British Isles by Mill Stephenson.* Ashford: Headley Brothers, 1938.

See also:

- HAINES, H. *A manual of monumental brasses, containing an introduction to the study of these memorials and a list of those remaining the British Isles.* 1961. Reprinted Bath: Adams & Dart, 1970.
- PAGE-PHILLIPS, I. *Macklin's monumental brasses.* 2nd ed. George Allen & Unwin, 1972.

CHAPTER FIVE

Inheritance, the Strict Settlement, and Marriage Settlements

A. Introduction

The status of a gentleman was normally based on his possession of landed property, which, preferably, he had inherited from his father or other close relative. The wider kin had little if any interest in the family estate, except when the direct line failed. Established families sought to emphasise their descent. Inherited wealth conferred respectability and a claim to deference. The 'one principal object' of the gentleman, according to Stone[98], was to preserve the link between the house, the estates to support it financially, and the family name. Many of the life choices of gentry family members were dependent on this basic imperative. Yes, daughters had to be married off. Yes, younger sons had to be provided for. But above all, the principal family estate had to be preserved intact for the benefit of the heirs of the eldest son. Sir Roger Wilbraham, writing in 1598, argued that a gentleman should organise his estate so that it could survive the four 'casualties' which were likely to strike it every few years. These casualties were lawsuits, building costs, service of the prince, and 'marrying a daughter'[99].

The task Wilbraham set was not necessarily easy. The landowner was subject to conflicting pressures, and had limited options. He frequently only possessed a life interest in his family's estate, and had no power to raise capital by selling lands. Gentlemen could find themselves with excessive debts. Sir Charles Kemeys, for example, owed £35,000 at his death in 1735[100]. Sometimes, drastic action was needed to raise cash.

The basic principal of inheritance law in most parts of England was primogeniture. Land was inherited by the eldest surviving son, or, in his absence, by daughters. Within that principal, the aim of preserving family estates down through the generations was met by the entail, a deed which 'settled the succession of an estate inalienably upon the descendants of an individual owner, in a specifically described order of preference'[101]. By this deed, the heir became merely a tenant for life, unable to sell his landed property. It was vested in trustees, who held it in trust for generations to come.

There were various types of entail. Medieval forms had been undermined by statute and legal judgement by the mid-sixteenth century. For the succeeding century, landowners enjoyed exceptional liberty to dispose of their lands as they wished. That situation changed in the latter half of the seventeenth century, with the development of the strict settlement.

Strict settlement was a legal device created to prevent the dissolution of an estate following a wastrel heir, a string of minorities, too many daughters, or the various other 'casualties' that could be inflicted upon an estate. It prevented the heir from selling the family estate, whilst allowing him to make provision for the 'casualties' that might occur. It also enabled the settlor to alter the succession of heirs if he wished (although primogeniture was nevertheless normally adhered to). Strict settlements helped to ensure that the ultimate catastrophe of the sale of on old family seat was a rare event, to be talked about and lamented for years thereafter. It formed the legal basis for the extraordinarily long survival of many large family estates.

B. The Strict Settlement

The Civil War and interregnum caused the gentry a great deal of anxiety. Royalists in particular had to spend much time defending their property against forfeitures and fines. They sought to develop legal devices which shielded them from the depredations of the Interregnum regime. This mind-set continued after the Restoration, with the development of the strict settlement. It quickly became the norm amongst all sectors of the gentry[102]. Settlements made the heir to an estate merely the tenant for life, not the outright owner. The property in question was vested in trustees, who were required to let it to the heir. The long-term interest of the family in the property was thereby secured against both punitive fines from the government, the incompetence of heirs, and the demands of lenders. By the eighteenth century, perhaps half of English land was held under settlements. The system continued throughout the nineteenth century[103].

Several copies of settlements were usually made; the parties, the trustees, and the lawyers, all needed to be able to consult them. In Yorkshire, Middlesex, and the Hatfield levels, copies were deposited in the local deeds registries[104]. Settlement deeds frequently survive amongst family muniments, and can be found in most record offices. They are long, verbose, and sometimes difficult to follow. But they are also mines of genealogical information. They set out in great detail how the main estate should descend, taking into account all possible contingencies, even down to unborn children. All possible heirs are named, so that not only sons, grandsons, and daughters are listed, but also uncles and distant cousins who might succeed fifty years later if the main line failed. The habit of drawing up family pedigrees mentioned in chapter 3 was not just for the sake of family pride, but also to help determine who should inherit. Virtually all were drawn up on the patrilineal principle: inheritance did not pass through women, unless there were no male descendants or relatives.

The strict settlement, sometimes referred to as the family settlement, was usually made when the heir came of age, when he married, or when the settlor died. A wide range of other events could also prompt a settlor to execute a deed. The unexpected birth of an heir, a severe illness, the inheritance of lands not covered by a settlement: these were just a few of the circumstances which persuaded settlors that action was needed.

If a settlement was made at death, it was made by will. Using the procedure of probate had the advantage that the testator could revoke the will during his life-time, and was not bound by it. However, a will could not alter a strict settlement unless that settlement granted the testator the power to do so.

Strict settlement, despite its name, was flexible. It could be broken, but only by collusive action between father and heir. Usually, once in a generation, it was in their interests to break the settlement, and to make a new one. When fathers needed to raise money to give their younger sons a start in life, or to give their daughters dowries, their eldest son needed an annuity to support himself - and his wife and children if he had them - until he inherited. Father and son would therefore collude to break the settlement, to pay off debts, and to raise money by selling off peripheral properties. A new settlement would be made, and the old one annulled. The parties to the deed would normally be the father and the son, together with both old and new trustees.

Strict settlements are frequently both lengthy and bulky documents. The scriveners who wrote them were paid by the number of words they contained, so it is not surprising that they are verbose[105]. It is therefore important to know what to expect in a deed before you read it. The important clauses are usually introduced by standard terminology written in capitals, eg 'TO HAVE AND TO HOLD'. Such clauses are easily picked out in documents which might otherwise be extremely difficult to read.

The major clauses in a deed of settlement are as follows[106]:

- *The Premises*. These give details of the names and ranks or occupations of the parties, who normally include the settlor, members of his family, and the trustees. The trustees of the previous settlement are likely to be named, as well as new trustees.
- *Recitals*. Settlements usually recite the previous settlement and other related deeds, establishing the settlor's title to the property, and giving details of any encumbrances on it. Each deed recited is usually prefaced by the word 'WHEREAS'.
- *The testatum*. This explains the purpose of the settlement, commencing with the word 'WITNESSETH', giving the reason for making the deed (frequently on the grounds of 'natural love and affection'), and listing the 'parcels' of property that are to be settled. The latter are prefaced by the words 'ALL THAT'. The property in question does not necessarily include all of the family's land; some may have been excluded in order to allow for greater flexibility in the settlor's management of his property. Outlying or newly acquired property could be sold or mortgaged to raise money without compromising possession of the main estate.
- *The habendum*. This clause usually begins with the words 'TO HAVE AND TO HOLD', and creates the 'uses' to which income from the estate is to be directed. After dealing with the settlor's own income, it may create separate trusts to pay an annuity to the heir, pin money and jointures to the wives of the settlor and his heir, and portions to younger children. The length of the settlement generally depended upon the complexity of the uses mentioned in it.
- *The entail*. The entail is probably the most important part of a settlement, certainly in the long term. It provides for the inheritance of the estate, and is therefore crucial for the family historian. Detailed family pedigrees could easily be constructed, without the need for other evidence, from the information provided in successive family settlements. The settlor is made a life tenant of the estate, and his eldest son the 'tenant in tail'. The deed then sets out the order of succession, listing the heirs' children one by one, then his brothers and their children, perhaps his sisters and their children, then uncles and cousins to the nth degree, finally ending with the 'right heirs'. The law would determine who they were, by applying the rules of primogeniture.
- *Trustees' powers*. A variety of powers could be granted to trustees, perhaps to exercise in conjunction with the settlor and/or his heir. They were likely to have the power to pay annuities, pin money, jointures, and portions. They could exercise the right to make or renew leases of the family's property, and to mortgage or sell particular pieces of land. They had to maintain the balance between the interests of the life tenant and the interests of the tenant in tail, and this was likely to be written into the settlement. Frequently, for example, they were forbidden to exact entry fines when making leases. If they did so, the rent payable would be reduced, and the life tenant would benefit at the cost of his heir.

- *Testimonium*. The final clause, prefaced with the words 'In witness whereof', included the signatures and seals of all the parties, and of witnesses to the deed. It is worth making a note of the latter; they may be lawyers, but, equally, they could be relatives or family friends.

The settlement could not be broken until the tenant in tail came of age, unless a private act of Parliament was procured. Once the tenant in tail was of age, he could join with the life tenant (normally his father) to break the entail by suffering a common recovery. This was a fictitious action in the Court of Common Pleas. The life tenant of an estate would bring an action against the tenant in tail to recover his lands. The latter would name a third party - the (frequently fictitious) common vouchee - to warrant his title in court. The vouchee, however, defaulted by not appearing to defend the tenant in tail's title. Judgement would therefore go to the life tenant, who would be free to make a new settlement. This would enable the tenant in tail - the heir - to secure provision for his maintainance in the form of an annuity or lands. The process could be continually repeated by each succeeding generation. Common recoveries can be found enrolled in TNA, classes CP40 (15th c.-1582) and CP43 (1583-1834). Indexes are available in IND1/17183-17216. Exemplifications of recoveries can sometimes be found amongst estate archives. An alternative to the common recovery was the fine, which is discussed below[107].

Settlements had the additional advantage that they protected family estates against any disabilities that the life tenant suffered from. Creditors could not break the settlement of a bankrupt life tenant. The heirs of a lunatic or a felon were protected against the dangers that their estate might otherwise fall into. If a life tenant committed treason, or suffered an attainder, and thus made himself liable to the loss of all his goods, the settlement protected his estate for his heir. The Earl of Derwentwater, for example, was deprived of his head for his participation in the 1745 rebellion. The title was not passed to his heir, but his estates were settled, and his son was allowed to inherit his lands[108]. Similarly, George Barclay of Dorking went bankrupt in 1803, owing c.£300,000. His creditors could not touch the £1500 per annum which had previously been settled on his children[109]. Settlements were sacrosanct to the government. The only way in which they could be broken, other than by collusion between life tenant and tenant in tail, was by act of Parliament.

Private acts of Parliament were expensive to procure, and were consequently only sought when wide acres were at stake. During the eighteenth and early nineteenth centuries, between 20 and 30 private estate acts were passed every year[110]. Prior to 1815, they were not officially printed. After this date, they were usually printed with other acts of Parliament, and can be consulted in major reference libraries. Unofficial copies can occasionally be found amongst family archives in local record offices.

Copies of all private acts are held by the House of Lords Record Office. For details, consult:

- Chronological Table of Private and Personal Acts
  www.opsi.gov.uk/chron-tables/private

Further Reading

- ENGLISH, BARBARA, & SAVILLE, JOHN. *Strict settlement: a guide for historians.* Occasional papers in economic and social history 10. Hull University Press, 1983.

C. Marriage Settlements

The marriage settlement was another important document in the process of inheritance. Sometimes, it was a full family settlement, concerned not just with the marriage, but with the descent of the whole estate. The majority of marriage settlements, however, were focused solely on making provision for the bride. Many letters, diaries, and other memoranda survive amongst family archives recording the delicate and sometimes prolonged negotiations concerning marriages. The aim of the father of an eligible young bachelor was to negotiate an alliance with a family of equal or perhaps superior status, who could provide a substantial dowry. Frequently the bride selected was a widow: 37% of the widows in a sample of wills from the Prerogative Court of Canterbury between 1500 and 1588 had been married at least twice[111]. The two families frequently lived some distance from each other; in 1642, only 44% of the alliances of Worcestershire gentry families were made with families native to that shire. Worcestershire may have been exceptional, but even in Kent, which was noted for its insularity, 18% of alliances were made outside of the county[112]. If you are searching for gentry marriage entries in parish registers[113], you may have to search in far distant places. It could be easier to find a marriage settlement. On the other hand, gentry marriages were frequently given much greater prominence in parish registers than those of their inferiors; much more information may be given than is usual.

Most gentry marriages were accompanied by marriage settlements; no landed family wanted its daughters to marry without one, since to do so could leave her at the mercy of an unscrupulous groom or his family. Under common law, all widows had the right to one-third of their husband's lands as dower. However, a jointure provided by a marriage settlement provided greater certainty and more flexibility than the dower provided by common law. If a jointure was provided, then the right to dower lapsed.

The parties to a marriage settlement were the bride and groom, together with trustees representing both families. If the bride and/or groom were merely heirs to the property being conveyed, their parents or other benefactors would be named. If the settlement involved the purchase of property, then the previous owner of that property would also be named. A marriage settlement commences with a recital of the fact that a marriage is to take place, and sometimes the amount of the dowry paid. The fact that a dowry is not mentioned does not necessarily mean that one was not paid.

The property mentioned in a marriage settlement did not necessarily include the entire estate or inheritance of the groom. However, it was likely to include all the bride's property. In law, everything she owned became her husband's property on marriage. The property in the settlement was assigned to trustees for the joint use of husband and wife or the survivor of them, and for their (unborn) children, or, in the absence of the latter, to the 'right heirs'.

The property involved in a marriage settlement was not necessarily land. Sarah Peters brought £20,000 in consols to her marriage with Thomas Brockhurst Barclay esq., in 1820. Her husband's life was to be insured for £5000. Memoranda on the original settlement deed show how the consols were subsequently sold and the money re-invested. Another memoranda accompanying the deed shows that the life insurance on her husband's life was paid up in 1866, when she received £9875[114].

9. Memorandum re sale of consols on the verso of a Barclay deed.

The principal seat generally changed hands only at death, when it would pass to either the eldest son, or to heiresses. Other parts of the estate might be temporarily alienated, for a variety of reasons. Widows were frequently entitled to dower rights for term of their lives. Property might be alienated to younger sons, or as daughters' dowries. Property might also be passed to trustees for the use of individual family members. The designation of heirs as tenants for life only was designed to ensure that property continued to be held by the family in perpetuity. The sale of property, especially the principal seat, meant the failure of family strategy.

Further Reading

- BONFIELD, LLOYD. *Marriage settlements, 1601-1740: the adoption of the strict settlement.* Cambridge University Press, 1983.

D. The Importance of Surnames

Gentlemen sought to identify themselves closely with their seat. Long residence in the same place enhanced a family's standing. Some gentlemen even took their names from their seats, for example, the Widdringtons of Widdrington (Northumberland), and the Fulfords of Fulford (Devon). Conversely, some gentlemen gave their names to their seats, or sometimes to other property that they owned. The latter practice dated back to Norman times. Many places with the same name were differentiated by the names of owners. Sampford Courteney and Sampford Peverell are two Devon examples, Charlton Musgrove and Charlton Adam are two from Somerset. Many new houses were given the name of its owner; the naming of Buckingham Palace is perhaps the best known example of this practice, albeit its builder, the Duke of Buckingham, was an aristocrat rather than a gentleman.

Great importance was attached to the perpetuation of the family name. The English practice whereby bride's surnames were obliterated at marriage gave surnames much less chance of survival than was the case on the continent, where women frequently retained their original family name. If the male line died out, the surname died out. And male lines of the gentry frequently did die out. The remedy adopted was the invention of fictive kin. Wills frequently required heirs to adopt the surname of the testator. The husbands of heiresses could be required to change their name in order to perpetuate their wives' maiden names. Heirs through the female line were frequently required to do the same. It has been calculated that some 10% of the landed elite changed their names after 1750[115].

Name changes were frequently accompanied by the even more symbolic adoption of the benefactor's coat of arms. Fictive kin could give the impression of lineal descent.

The ancient family of Widdrington of Widdrington (Northumberland) only kept their surname in the nineteenth century by heiresses marrying husbands who were prepared to change their names[116]. Consequently, their Cook and Jackson names were lost.

Of course, the requirement to change ones name in order to inherit was not always popular with the heir. If he was of distinctly inferior rank and income, then the symbolism might be perceived as being worth the cost. If, however, he was of superior rank and income, then the loss of his own family name would be felt much more strongly. After all, he would be just as keen to preserve his own family name as his benefactor was to preserve his.

There were alternative strategies to a straight-forward change of name. Some heirs simply added the new surname to their own, creating the double-barrelled surname - or sometimes the triple-barrelled surname - which became so common amongst the gentry. This solution meant that the coat of arms could be added to, rather than replaced. When Sir Thomas Gower, Bt., married the coheiress of Sir John Leveson, he named his second son William Leveson-Gower, clearly intending to establish a new family based on the Leveson estate. He failed: William's elder brother died childless, and the estate reverted to William - who retained his double-barrelled surname[117].

Hyphenation of surnames had the disadvantage that it could not be done repeatedly. Four hyphenated surnames was the absolute maximum, although it became common for those with over-hyphenated surnames to use the final surname by itself.

An alternative device was to give the wife's surname to children as a forename. When a Mildmay heiress married a Fane in 1629, the first-born son was named Mildmay[118]. This was not, however, a secure way of maintaining the name. Mildmay Fane's eldest son was not given the name, although a younger son was. In the next generation the name disappeared from view.

There was, and is, no legal requirement to record a change of name. However, it is likely that gentry who changed their names in order to inherit would have recorded that change in a legal document. Name changes could be made by Act of Parliament, although this was an expensive procedure, and only likely when there was a valuable estate to be inherited. The means to trace acts has already been discussed.

A much cheaper procedure was to apply for a royal licence. This was frequently done when an inheritance depended on a name change, a marriage settlement required a husband to adopt his wife's surname, or a name change involved adopting a benefactor's coat of arms. The earliest royal licence dates from 1679. They were increasingly used as alternatives to acts of Parliament, which became rare after c.1770. After 1783, all requests for royal licences were referred to the College of Arms for approval (which was never denied)[119].

Warrants for royal licences can be found in TNA, classes SP 44 (until 1782), HO 38 (1782 to 1868), and HO 142 (1868 onwards). They were also advertised in the *London gazette,* although this was not invariable. It may be searched online at:

- Gazettes
  www.london-gazette.co.uk

An even less expensive method of evidencing a change of name was to execute a deed poll. This is a legal contract involving only one party. Between 1851 and 1903, these could be enrolled on the Close Rolls, held by TNA (class C54 for 1851-1903; class J18 2903-2003). This was not always done. Many deed polls were executed without being enrolled.

Many (but not all) changes of names recorded in these sources between 1760 and 1903 are indexed in:

- PHILLIMORE, W. P. W., & FRY, E. A. *An index to changes of name under authority of acts of Parliament or royal licence, and including irregular changes from 1 George III to 64 Victoria, 1760 to 1901.* Phillimore & Co., 1905. Reprinted Baltimore: Genealogical Publishing Co., 1968.

For more information on changes of name, consult the TNA research guide:

- Change of Name
  www.nationalarchives.gov.uk/records/research-guides/change-of-name.htm

It is important to recognise that changes of spelling are not necessarily changes of name. Names were frequently spelt in a variety of different ways, depending on the clerk who was recording them. In the fourteenth century, Chief Justice Shareshull is known to have spelt his name in at least 107 different ways[120]. The gentry were just as prone as other ranks of society to give different versions of the same name.

CHAPTER SIX
Estate and Legal Records of the Gentry

A. General

Every gentleman's house had a muniment room, or at least a chest, for containing all the documents required for efficient running of an estate. At the core of the muniments were the deeds which proved title to all the property on the estate (including settlements). Then there were the tenants' leases, which showed legal entitlement to rents. Many estates were surveyed to provide an overall picture of estate management. Surveys might be accompanied by maps. Rentals acted as aide memoires to show what rent was due when. Rents received, and other income, were recorded in accounts, as were outgoings such as servants' wages. Fathers might prepare books of advice for their heirs. Pedigrees might serve to strengthen title to both land and status. Wills - both those which were proved, and those which were superseded by later wills - may be found. A variety of other records were kept, for example, journals, letters, shop books, and records of litigation. All of these documents are of interest to the family historian. Many collections of family archives have been deposited in local record offices, in the British Library, and in a variety of other institutions.

A wide variety of estate records can also be found in TNA. Muniments relating to Crown estates, and to estates which came into the possession of the Crown, are held there. In particular, the monastic estates seized by Henry

VIII were administered by the Court of Augmentations, which merged with the Court of General Surveyors, and subsequently with the Exchequer. The records of these courts contain numerous deeds, rentals, surveys, etc.

Many deeds and other records were called in as evidence in legal cases, and remain in the archives of the central courts. The procedures of the courts were sometimes used to register deeds, and to secure a record that was beyond doubt. There were also local deeds registries in a small number of counties. The archives of boroughs also include many estate records, which may include information relating to the gentry.

A detailed listing of major collections of estate records can be found in:

* *Principal family and estate collections: family names A-[Z]*. 2 vols. Guides to sources for British history 10. HMSO, 1996.

B. Deeds

Deeds name the parties to a conveyance of land. In doing so, they usually provide information that is useful to family historians. At the least, a deed will give you a name, and usually a date, together with details of the property which the parties were interested in. Sometimes, they will give you much more than this.

A wide variety of different types of deeds may be encountered. Settlements have already been discussed. A detailed exposition of other deeds and their contents cannot be given here. Medieval deeds are normally in Latin, and require some expertise in palaeography to read. Some post-medieval deeds are also in Latin, although this ceased in 1733. Dates in deeds may be expressed in regnal years, and sometimes refer to saints days and other festivals. Amongst the more common types of post-medieval deeds were:

* The feoffment, which normally begins with the words, 'Sciant presentes et futuri' - 'Know for the present and future'. This was a development of the medieval practice known as livery of seizin, in which the vendor handed the purchaser a clod of earth from the property as the act of sale. The feoffment confirmed that livery had taken place. It was not an agreement between two parties, but a statement of what one of them had done.
* The bargain and sale was a development from the feoffment. When it was introduced in 1535, it did away with the need for livery of seizin to take place. The deed had to be enrolled either on the Close Rolls (TNA C54), or by the Clerk of the Peace in the relevant county.

- The Quitclaim was used to release rights in property to another. Sometimes they were endorsed with livery of seizin, and were used as feoffments. They are frequently in Latin, and commence with the words 'Omnibus Christi fidelibus - 'to all the faithful in Christ'.
- Fines are records of entirely fictitious legal cases, written to confirm changes of ownership, and enrolled in the Court of Common Pleas. They open with the words 'Hec est finalis concordia ...' - 'this is the final agreement ...'. The deforciant (the vendor) agrees to warrant the claim of the querent (the purchaser) to the property. It is frequently not clear what the purpose of a fine was; however, many purchaser's copies are accompanied by another deed which explain its purposes. The final concord, or fine, was prepared in triplicate, in a very archaic handwriting. It was always written in Latin until 1733. One copy was given to the vendor, one to the purchaser, and the final copy (the foot of the fine) was retained in the Court of Common Pleas (now in TNA, class CP25). There are separate series for the Palatinates of Cheshire (1307-1830, CHES31), Durham (1535-1834, DUR12), and Lancaster (1377-1834, PL17). Many record societies have published the feet of fines for their counties. A TNA information leaflet entitled 'Land conveyances: feet of fines 1182-1833' **www.nationalarchives.gov.uk/records/research-guides/land-conveyance-feet-of-fines.htm** gives more details. See also KISSOCK, JONATHAN. 'Medieval feet of fines: a study of their uses with a catalogue of published sources', *Local historian* **24**, 1994, pp.66-82. Fines were abolished in 1834.
- The lease and release was invented c.1600 as a means of avoiding the publicity involved in feoffments and bargain and sales. The property in question was leased to the purchaser for 12 months, putting him in possession. On the following day, the vendor released his interest in the property to the purchaser. This procedure avoided the need for enrolment or livery of seizin, as it only transferred an interest in the property, rather than the freehold. It became perhaps the commonest means of conveying property until legislation of 1845 ended its usefulness.
- Common recoveries have already been discussed[121]. They took the form of a fictitious court case, and were used to destroy the entails in settlements.
- Letters patent were used for royal grants of land - especially for grants of former monastic property, and for alienations of land held directly from the Crown. They are enrolled on the patent rolls (TNA C66), which have been calendared up to 1578 in the *Patent rolls of the reign of Henry III ... AD 1216-1235* (HMSO, 1901), and succeeding volumes. Entries on these rolls provide detailed descriptions of the property concerned, sometimes based on valuations made for prospective purchasers now in the 'Particulars for grants' (TNA E318), which themselves are based on surveys of monastic properties. The latter are listed in *List of Rentals and surveys and other analogous documents.* Lists and indexes **25**. (HMSO, 1901; reprinted Kraus Reprint, 1963), and also in *List of Rentals and Surveys: Addenda. Lists and Indexes to No. XXV.* Lists and indexes, Supplementary Series, **14**. (Kraus

Reprint Corporation, 1968). For a collection of these documents relating to Devon, see YOUINGS, JOYCE, ed. *Devon monastic lands: calendar of particulars for grants 1536-1558*. (Devon & Cornwall Record Society, New series 1, 1955). Similar documents to letters patent are also enrolled in the charter rolls (TNA C53) for the period 1199-1517. These have been calendared for 1226-1417 in the *Calendar of the charter rolls preserved in the Public Record Office*. 5 vols. HMSO, 1903-1916.

- The mortgage began as a lease for a long period at a nominal rent, granted for a specific sum of money. If that money was repaid with interest by a fixed date, the lease would be cancelled. If not, it would become 'absolute', and the mortgagee would become the owner of the property. The lessor retained possession of the property, although that is not stated in the deed. Sometimes, the mortgage was accompanied by a bond, which bound the lessor to pay a fixed sum by a certain date, or forfeit twice the amount. This offered an alternative to foreclosure. It became a popular way of raising money in the seventeenth century and later.
- Copyhold land was held by copy of court roll. Whilst this was a servile tenure, in practice gentlemen could and did hold land by this means, and copies can be found amongst estate papers. Nevertheless, it is easier to find evidence of copyhold land by consulting manorial court rolls directly (see below).

Many deeds were enrolled in the records of the central law courts. Details can be found in TNA's guide to land conveyances noted below. There were also a few deeds registries in the provinces. Where these existed, it should be possible to use them to trace all land transactions from the date they were established. For details, see:

- SHEPPARD, F., & BELCHER, F. 'The deeds registries of Yorkshire and Middlesex', *Journal of the Society of Archivists* 6(5), 1980, pp.274-286.
- West Riding Registry of Deeds
  www.archives.wyjs.org.uk/wyjs-archives-w-r-registry-d.asp
- East Riding Register of Deeds
  www.eastriding.gov.uk/cs/culture-and-information/archives/sources-we-hold (click title).
- The Middlesex Deeds Registry
  www.cityoflondon.gov.uk/NR/rdonlyres/E69300BA-9550-4705-8534- 01896C87A54E/0/LH_LMA_middlesexdeeds.PDF

Deeds in estate archives frequently come in bundles, with an abstract for the whole bundle, which is worth checking first. Such bundles may provide all the evidence you need to trace the descent of a particular property through many decades or perhaps centuries. Most of the deeds are likely to be endorsed with details of their contents, so you know which ones are most likely to be relevant.

Further Reading

An excellent introduction to titles deeds is provided by:

* WORMLEIGHTON, TIM. *Title deeds for family historians.* Family History Partnership, 2012.

For a more detailed guide, see:

* ALCOCK, N. W. *Old title deeds: a guide for local and family historians.* 2nd ed. Phillimore, 2001.

Other useful works include:

* DIBBEN, A.A. *Title deeds, 13th-19th centuries.* Helps for students of history **72.** Rev ed. Historical Association, 1990.
* CORNWALL, JULIAN. *An introduction to ... reading old title deed.* 2nd ed. FFHS, 1997.
* Land Conveyances: enrolment of deeds and registration of title **www.nationalarchives.gov.uk/records/research-guides/land-conveyances-deeds-title.htm**
* How to Interpret Deeds: a simple guide and glossary **www.britishrecordsassociation.org.uk/pages/guide3.htm**

For an online collection of medieval deeds, see:

* Deeds Project **www.utoronto.ca/deeds**

Numerous abstracts of deeds have been published by record societies and others. See, for example:

* PUGH, R. B., ed. *A calendar of Antrobus deeds to 1624.* Wiltshire Archaeological and Natural History Society, Records Branch, **3.** 1947.

For the legal background to deeds and other estate records, see:

* SIMPSON, A. W. B. *An introduction to the history of the land law.* Oxford University Press, 1961.

C. Manorial Records

Most estates were composed of a number of manors, each of which held its own manorial court. These might be conducted by the lord himself, or by his steward. Manorial records survive from the twelfth century until as late as 1925 (when copyhold tenure was abolished), although complete runs of court rolls are rare. The rolls of the Manor of Wakefield (Yorkshire) which covered much of the West Riding, are exceptional both chronologically and topographically; many have been published by the Yorkshire Archaeological Society **www.wakecourtroll.yas.org.uk**.

The manorial court met at regular intervals, according to local custom. The Court Baron regulated the manor's agricultural practice, rights and duties of lords and tenants, tenurial changes, and disputes between tenants. The Court Leet and View of Frankpledge dealt with the election of officers such as reeves and constables, and felonies such as breaches of the peace and theft.

The proceedings of manorial courts were recorded on court rolls. They record the descent of tenancies from father to son, and so contain a great deal of valuable genealogical information. There may also be accounts, surveys, and a variety of other estate records, which will be discussed below. The value of these records for the family history of the gentry is that they enable us to see gentry estates as they actually worked. Manorial records are of limited use for tracing gentry genealogy. They do enable us to identify stewards, who may have been upwardly mobile gentry. It is also worth remembering that tenants were not just yeomen and husbandmen; they could be gentlemen too, renting out property which rounded off their other estates. In 1517, no less a person than Sir Edward Hungerford of Farleigh Castle (Somerset) was fined for his absence from Bradford on Avon's manorial court[122].

Manorial court rolls can be located by consulting the Manorial Documents Register **www.nationalarchives.gov.uk/mdr**. This is described in:

- Manorial Documents Register and Manorial Lordships
  www.nationalarchives.gov.uk/records/research-guides/manorial-documents-register-lordships.htm

There are two useful TNA research guides:

- Manorial Records
  www.nationalarchives.gov.uk/records/research-guides/manorial-records.htm
- Manor and other local court rolls, 13th century to 1922
  www.nationalarchives.gov.uk/records/research-guides/manor-court-rolls.htm

Valuable introductions are provided by:

- ELLIS, MARY. *Using manorial records.* 2nd ed. Readers guide **6**. Public Record Office, 1999.
- HARVEY, P. D. A. *Manorial records.* Archives & the user **5**. British Records Association, 1984.

D. Wills and Probate

Wills and other probate records are major sources for all genealogists. They are particularly important for tracing the gentry, and may provide a great deal of detail. Normally, all living children are mentioned; perhaps grandchildren as well. Wills also give the names of executors, who normally inherited the residue of estates after all the legacies had been disposed of, together with the signatures of witnesses. Unlike the wills of the lower classes, gentry wills are likely to go much further, with legacies to servants, cousins, neighbours, and others. They paint a picture of the social milieu in which the gentry moved.

Sometimes, wills were used to make a strict settlement of the estate. The religious clauses provide another feature, which may tell us something about the beliefs of the testator, and perhaps whether he was a puritan or a Roman Catholic. These clauses must be examined closely; they are not necessarily all that they seem. They may reflect the opinions of the scribe, or be inserted because that is the done thing. However, literate gentry were perhaps more likely to influence these clauses than were testators of a lower class.

A number of other documents may be found filed with wills. Executors had to produce an inventory of the deceased's estate, which paints a picture of his mode of living, with details of the furniture in his house, the crops in his fields, the horses in his stables, perhaps the books in his library, and all the other goods which a gentleman might acquire.

The administration bond provides rather less information. It required the executor or administrator to faithfully administer the estate, giving his name, perhaps the name of a friend or relative who stood bound with him, and the name of the official granting probate. It might also require the executor to make provision for children's education, or for a widow's maintenance. And it might require him to produce an account of his administration.

Administration accounts may occasionally be found with other probate records. They record the amount that has come into the hands of the executor or administrator, and the amount he has expended. The former is usually the amount of the inventory; the later includes legacies, funeral expense, debts, and other expenses that may have been incurred. They may give a much more detailed picture of an estate than the inventory alone.

Wills generally had to be proved in ecclesiastical courts, and now survive in diocesan archives, which can usually be found in local record offices. Most wills were proved in local archdeaconry courts. If, however, you had goods in two archdeaconries, jurisdiction went to the diocesan consistory courts. If your goods were in two different dioceses, jurisdiction was with either the Prerogative Court of Canterbury (PCC), or its equivalent in York. In practice, the gentry frequently proved their wills in the most prestigious court, that is, the PCC.

Details of the numerous different courts where wills were proved, and of the record offices which hold probate records, can be found in:

- GIBSON, JEREMY, & CHURCHILL, ELSE. *Probate jurisdictions: where to look for wills*. 5th ed. Federation of Family History Societies, 2002.

For more information, especially about PCC records, visit:

- Wills and Probate Records
  www.nationalarchives.gov.uk/records/research-guides/wills-and-probate-records.htm

PCC wills are now online at:

- Wills 1384-1858
  www.nationalarchives.gov.uk/records/wills.htm

Most wills are only likely to survive in the archives of probate courts. However, gentlemen frequently retained copies of their wills, including wills which had not been proved, or which had been superseded. These can now sometimes be found in family collections of estate records. Abstracts from wills were required by the administrators of death duties, which are discussed below[123].

Only a brief summary of information relating to probate records can be given here. For a much more detailed guide, consult:

- RAYMOND, STUART A. *The wills of our ancestors: the family and local historian's guide to probate records*. Pen & Sword, 2012.

See also:

- GRANNUM, KAREN, & TAYLOR, NIGEL. *Wills & probate records: a guide for family historians.* 2nd ed. National Archives, 2009.

Many collections of probate records have been edited and published by record societies and others[124]. See, for example:

- BELL, PATRICIA, ed. *Bedfordshire wills 1484-1533.* Bedfordshire Historical Record Society **76**. 1997.
- WANKLYN, MALCOLM, ed. *Inventories of Worcestershire landed gentry, 1537-1786.* Worcestershire Historical Society New Series **16**. 1998.

E. Debt

There were many occasions when gentlemen had to borrow money. It might be needed, for example, to pay daughters' dowries, to fund litigation, or to pay off substantial debts. Debts were not necessarily evidence of imprudence: losses could be incurred in a variety of ways other than extravagance. Sir Edward Stradling's debts amounting to £21,000 were probably caused by his losses in the Civil War; when they caused him to default on a huge bond, he brought down the Bassetts of Beaupre and the Vans of Marcross with him, since they had stood surety for him. Their fall was not typical of gentle families; most landed families in Glamorganshire continually battled with debt, but most had sufficient resources to survive[125].

We have already seen how long-term loans could be raised by mortgage from the seventeenth century onwards. Smaller sums could easily be raised by recognizances (sometimes referred to as bonds), whereby a borrower entered into an agreement to pay a fixed sum by a certain date, with penal clauses in case of default. From 1532, these recognizances were enrolled by the Clerk of the Recognizances. Recognizance rolls are preserved as class LC4 in TNA. Unfortunately, there are no indexes.

Writs for the recovery of debt were issued by a number of courts. Those for the Court of Chancery can be found in TNA C131 and C239; for the Duchy of Lancaster in DL23. These sometimes include inventories - known as 'extents for debts' - of the goods of defaulting mercantile debtors. Those for London are listed in:

- CARLIN, MARTHA, ed. *London and Southwark inventories 1316-1650: a handlist of extents for debts.* Centre for Metropolitan History, Institute of Historical Research, University of London, 1997.

Debt was an imprisonable offence. The bankruptcy laws were developed in order to mitigate its consequences. From 1571, conveyances of bankrupts' estates had to be enrolled on the Close rolls (TNA C54) after 1571. For the records of bankrupts after 1710, consult:

- Bankrupts and Insolvent Debtors 1710-1869
  www.nationalarchives.gov.uk/records/research-guides/bankrupts-insolvent-1710-1869.htm

F. Other Estate Records

Accounts, rentals, surveys, and maps are frequently found in estate archives. They provide snapshots of estates at particular dates. Manorial accounts showed the various financial transactions in a manor during a specified period, and reveal how much the steward was due to pay to his lord, or vice versa. If all the property of a manor was leased out, accounts may just show the names of tenants and the rent they paid. Tenants are also listed by rentals, which also show the property they tenanted, and the amount of the rent paid. Sometimes, there are series of rentals, enabling the succession of tenants to be easily established.

Surveys are similar documents, but are also likely to include information about tenure, including details of entry fines, dates of leases, etc. They may also record acreages, land use, buildings, and other information likely to help the landlord to determine future estate policy. For example, the Aclands owned the manor of Efford, near Stratton (Cornwall). Their c.1800 survey shows that 'a cottage late Row', in Launcells (Cornwall) was leased to Wrey Ians, esq., for 5s[126]. Ians leased several other properties from the Aclands, and was himself a substantial landowner in the area. Some of the Acland surveys are accompanied by estate maps. Such maps are frequently the earliest large-scale maps for the area covered. Surveys were frequently made on changes of ownership, when the new owner wanted to discover the value of his estate, and to work out ways in which his income might be enhanced.

Rentals and surveys are valuable sources for tracing the history of estate ownership, and for assessing the value of an estate to its lord. They may also provide information about gentlemen who leased parts of their estates from other gentlemen. Tenants were not necessarily just yeomen and husbandmen. They could be gentlemen too.

G. Official Surveys

Extensive information about the ownership and occupation of land can be found in a number of important surveys that were conducted under official or semi-official auspices. The earliest such survey was Domesday Book, initiated by William the Conqueror in 1086. For the present purposes, the major surveys were enclosure awards, tithe apportionments, the *Return of owners of land*; and the Valuation Office survey authorised by the Finance Act 1909-1910.

In the medieval period, villeins frequently farmed their fields in common, and consequently many fields were unenclosed. This practice was increasingly considered to be inefficient, and landlords and tenants increasingly agreed to enclose their lands, and to create separate farms. The gentry were frequently the prime movers in encouraging enclosures. Between 1700 and 1900, about 7,000,000 acres of open fields were enclosed. The process of enclosure was carefully recorded in enclosure agreements and maps. These show the names of landowners (mostly gentry, although some gentry were also tenants) and tenants, and provide detailed information on their land holdings. Early agreements can frequently be found amongst the records of Chancery and other courts; subsequently, enclosure was frequently effected by private Acts of Parliament, until the General Enclosure Act 1836 made this unnecessary. Copies of enclosure awards and maps were made for the Clerk of the Peace, and to be kept in the parish chest; these can now be found in local record offices. Some are also held in TNA. For an introduction to these records, see TNA's research guide:

- Enclosure Awards
  www.nationalarchives.gov.uk/records/research-guides/enclosure.htm

For a more detailed guide, see:

- HOLLOWELL, STEVEN. *Enclosure records for historians.* Phillimore, 2000.

Enclosure records are listed in:

- TATE, W. E. *A domesday of English enclosure acts and awards.* University of Reading Library, 1978.

Between the eighth and the nineteenth centuries, the Biblical injunction to give a tenth of one's income to the service of God was a legal obligation. Tithes were frequently a bone of contention between parishioners and parochial incumbents. The Quakers refused to pay them. The Tithe Commutation Act 1836 converted tithes into a rent payment based on the price of grain, It required the compilation of tithe awards, listing landowners and tenants, and tithe maps, showing the property they owned or tenanted. These records survive for no less than 11,395 English and Welsh parishes and townships, and effectively provide a census of householders. A brief introduction to these records is provided by a TNA research guide:

- Tithe Records
  www.nationalarchives.gov.uk/records/research-guides/tithe-records.htm

For a more detailed introduction, see:

- EVANS, ERIC J., & CROSBY, ALAN G. *Tithes: maps, apportionments, and the 1836 act: a guide for local historians*. 3rd ed. British Association for Local History, 1997.

Tithe maps are listed in:

- KAIN, ROGER J. P., & OLIVER, RICHARD R, *The tithe maps of England and Wales: a cartographic analysis and county-by-county catalogue.* Cambridge University Press, 1995.

TNA's holdings of maps and apportionments are listed in:

- *Inland Revenue tithe maps and apportionments (IR29, IR30)*. 2 vols. List and Index Society **68** & **83**. 1971-2.

The land question was another major issue in the nineteenth century. The *Return of owners of land 1873* was compiled by the government and published as a Parliamentary paper (1874 vol.72). It lists everyone who owned more than one acre of land (except in London and Middlesex), and effectively serves as a census of gentry heads of households. Its information was derived from rate books. The return is available on a pay-per-view database **www.ancestry.co.uk**. Many county sections are also available on free online databases; see, for example:

- Return of Owners of Land in England and Wales
  http://uk-genealogy.org.uk/OwnersofLand.html

The land question continued to exercise the thoughts of politicians into the twentieth century. Lloyd George's Finance Act 1909-1910 launched what was probably the most extensive survey of land ownership and occupation ever attempted. The Valuation Office field books, now in TNA (class IR58) record the names of all landowners and occupiers, with detailed descriptions of each property. Valuation books, giving similar information, are held by county record offices. Maps showing hereditaments are in TNA, classes IR121-35. It should be possible to identify the landowners and occupiers in every parish.

A brief introduction to the Valuation Office records is provided by TNA's research guide:

- Valuation Office Records: The Finance (1909-1910) Act
  www.nationalarchives.gov.uk/records/research-guides/valuation-office-records.htm

See also:

- SHORT, BRIAN, & REED, MICK. 'An Edwardian land survey: the Finance (1909-10) Act 1910 Records', *Journal of the Society of Archivists*, **8**(2), 1986, pp.95-103. See also **8**(1), p82-3.
- SHORT, BRIAN M. 'The Lloyd George Finance Act material', in *Short guides to records, second series: guides 25-48*. Historical Association, 1997, pp.63-69.

A more extensive guide is provided by:

- SHORT, BRIAN. *Land and society in Edwardian Britain*. Cambridge University Press, 1997.

A detailed guide to both tithe maps and apportionments, and the Valuation Office survey, is provided by:

- BEECH, GERALDINE, & MITCHELL, ROSE, *Maps for family and local history: the records of the tithe, Valuation Office, and national farm surveys*. 2nd ed. National Archives, 2004.

H. Court Records

In contrast to the evidence provided by monumental inscriptions, the records of Chancery and other courts of law frequently depict the dark side of gentry life. The accusations made against opponents in court (which must sometimes be taken with a grain of salt) were frequently scurrilous, not to say libellous. Sir William Maurice of Clenennau was described in a Star Chamber suit as being 'a man of great power and authority ... a turbulent and contentious man amongst his neighbours and carrying a greedy mind unlawfully to enrich himself by other men's goods and lands'[127].

Litigation was a status disease for gentlemen. Many had some training in the law[128], and were ready to turn to the courts to remedy any dispute that arose with neighbours or relatives. Sir Richard Hawksworth of Hawksworth (Yorkshire), for example, was involved in at least 15 different law suits between 1632 and 1658. Just one of these cost him £500[129].

The records of the central courts have been described by Hoyle as 'too large, too rich, too compelling to be ignored'[130]. The rural gentry made extensive use of these courts. Medieval King's Bench records in particular tell us a great deal about them, their tenantry and officials, their feuds, and their legal or semi-legal activities. Court records are admittedly difficult to use, since many pre-1733 documents were written in Latin, and many are un-indexed. Nevertheless, some indexes do exist, some documents are in English, and the rewards for consulting these sources can be considerable. This is not the place to provide a detailed guide to these records, but a brief overview can be given.

Litigants had a wide range of courts in which to pursue their actions. There was a basic distinction between the common law and equity, which must be understood. The common law courts - Common Pleas, the Exchequer of Pleas, the King's Bench - were concerned with fact, but judgements in these courts could be rigid, harsh and inequitable; they did not recognise some types of property, for example, copyhold, mortgages, and uses, nor could the common law provide justice where deeds had been lost. Many litigants therefore petitioned the Crown to settle disputes equitably. That led to the growth of equity courts, primarily the Court of Chancery, but also Star Chamber, the Court of Requests, and the Court of Exchequer. Their aim was to settle disputes. Equity was concerned with motivation, rather than with the strict interpretation of formal documents. That meant, for example, that the mortgage became a secure means of credit, rather than a device by which lenders could seize the lands of their creditors.

10. Kings' Bench in session (Wikimedia).

Procedures varied in each court. In general, in the Common Law courts, proceedings were initiated by a writ, which could be purchased from the court, and pleadings were heard orally before a jury. In the equity courts, the plaintiff had to petition the court by a bill of grievance, normally in English. Evidence was gathered by interrogatory and deposition, and perhaps by replication (the defendant's reply to the plaintiff's deposition) and rejoinder (the plaintiff's response to the replication). These documents, and especially depositions, provide much valuable evidence for family historians. Equity cases were decided by a judge, who was able to mitigate the harshness of the common law.

Records of the central courts are held by TNA. They cannot be described here in detail. A variety of different guides are available, and are listed below. The Selden Society **www.selden-society.qmw.ac.uk** has published many legal records; so have a number of other record societies. Some of their publications are noted below, as are a number of List and Index Society **www.listandindexsociety.org.uk** calendars and indexes. For general guidance on medieval records of the common law, visit:

- Public Records: Common Law Records
  www.medievalgenealogy.org.uk/guide/leg.shtml

Court of Chancery

The records of Chancery are mostly in English, and a variety of indexes are available. A detailed guide is provided by:

- HORWITZ, HENRY. *Chancery equity records and proceedings, 1600-1800*. Public Record Office 1998.

There are also two guides written specifically for family historians:

- MOORE, SUSAN T. *Family feuds: an introduction to Chancery proceedings*. Federation of Family History Societies, 2003.
- GERHOLD, DORIAN. *Courts of Equity: a guide to Chancery and other legal records for local and family historians*. Pinhorns, 1994. Reprinted from *Local historian, 17*, 1987, pp.408-416 and 475-482.

Some sample pleadings are included in:

- HORWITZ, HENRY, & MORETON, CHARLES, eds. *Samples of Chancery pleadings & suits, 1627, 1685, 1735 and 1785*. List & Index Society **257**. 1995.

A number of TNA research guides are available:

- Chancery Proceedings: Equity Suits before 1558
  www.nationalarchives.gov.uk/records/research-guides/chancery-equity-before-1558.htm
- Chancery Proceedings: Equity Suits from 1558
  www.nationalarchives.gov.uk/records/research-guides/chancery-equity-from-1558.htm
- Chancery Masters Reports and Certificates
  www.nationalarchives.gov.uk/records/research-guides/chancery-masters-reports-certificates.htm
- Chancery Masters and other Exhibits
  www.nationalarchives.gov.uk/records/research-guides/chancery-masters-exhibits.htm

See also:

- Public Records: Chancery and other Equity Suits
  www.medievalgenealogy.org.uk/guide/cha.shtml

Some 30,000 Chancery pleadings, c.1625-1714, are included in:

- The Equity Pleadings Database
  www.nationalarchives.gov.uk/equity

Many Chancery proceedings are indexed in the Society of Genealogists' Bernau index. For a discussion of this index, see:

- SHARP, HILARY. *How to Use the Bernau Index.* 2nd ed. Society of Genealogists, 2000.

Court of Chivalry
This was a court of civil law, which heard many defamation cases, as well as contested claims to gentility and coats of arms. Few records survive. Those which do provide 'a rich source for the contemporary vocabulary of insult', as well as a wealth of biographical detail on plaintiffs, defendants and witnesses[131]. Many have been published by the Harleian Society. See:

- SQUIBB, D., ed. *Reports of heraldic cases in the Court of Chivalry, 1623-1732.*

Harleian Society **107**. 1956.

- CUST, RICHARD P., & HOPPER, ANDREW J., eds. *Cases in the High Court of Chivalry, 1634-1640*. Harleian Society new series **18**. 2006. This is accompanied by a website database:
- The Court of Chivalry
  www.court-of-chivalry.bham.ac.uk

For a detailed history of the Court, see:

- SQUIBB, G. D. *The High Court of Chivalry.: a study of the civil law in England.* Clarendon Press, 1959. This can be read at **www.questia.com/library/book/high-court-of-chivalry-a-study-of-the-civil-law-in-england-by-g-d-squibb.jsp**

Court of Common Pleas

The majority of property disputes were heard in the Court of Common Pleas. Unfortunately, its records are particularly difficult to use, and mostly unindexed. Its plea rolls are in TNA, class CP40; affidavits are in CP3. A variety of other records are also available, and can be identified through the TNA catalogue[132]. A transcript of fifteenth century plea rolls can be searched at:

- British History Online: Court of Common Pleas: The National Archives, CP40, 1399-1500
  www.british-history.ac.uk/source.aspx?pubid=1272

Court of Exchequer

A brief introduction to Exchequer equity proceedings is provided by a TNA research guide:

- Equity Proceedings in the Court of Exchequer
  www.nationalarchives.gov.uk/records/research-guides/equity-court-of-exchequer.htm

For more detailed guidance, consult:

- HORWITZ, HENRY. *Exchequer equity records and proceedings 1649-1841.* Handbook **32**. Public Record Office, 2001.

For some examples of pleadings, see:

- COOKE, JESSICA, & HORWITZ, HENRY, eds. *Samples of Exchequer equity pleadings and suits 1685-86, 1734-35 and 1818-19*. List & Index Society, **278**. 2000.
- HORWITZ, HENRY, & COOKE, JESSICA, eds. *London and Middlesex Exchequer equity pleadings, 1685-1686 and 1784-1785: a calendar*. London Record Society, **35**. 2000.

Court of Requests

TNA has provided a research guide to the records of this court:

- Court of Requests 1485-1642
  www.nationalarchives.gov.uk/records/research-guides/court-of-requests.htm

For some examples of records, see:

- LEADAM, I. S., ed. *Select Cases in the Court of Requests*. Selden Society, **12**, 1898.
- STRETTON, TIM, ed. *Marital litigation in the Court of Requests, 1542-1642*. Camden 5th series **32**. Royal Historical Society, 2008.

Court of Star Chamber

- Court of Star Chamber 1485-1642
  www.nationalarchives.gov.uk/records/research-guides/star-chamber.htm
- GUY, J. A. *The Court of Star Chamber and its records to the reign of Elizabeth I. Handbook 21.* HMSO, 1984. This is supplemented by:
- BARNES, T. G. 'The Archives and Archival Problems of the Elizabethan and Early Stuart Star Chamber', *Journal of the Society of Archivists*, 2, 1963, pp.345-360.

Various lists of Star Chamber proceedings are available:

- *List of proceedings in the Court of Star Chamber preserved in the Public Record Office, vol.1 (1485-1558)*. Lists and Indexes **13**. Kraus Reprint 1963.
- *Proceedings in the Court of Star Chamber*. 5 vols. Lists and Indexes, Supplementary series; 4, Kraus Reprint, 1966-1975. Contents Vol. 1. 1485-1558: Indexes to Lists and Indexes, No. 13. Vol. 2. Elizabeth I Index of persons in bundles A-C. Vol. 3. Elizabeth I, index of persons in bundles D-K. Vol. 4. Elizabeth I. Index of persons in bundles L-R. Vol. 5. Elizabeth I, index of persons in bundles S-Z.
- BARNES, THOMAS GARDEN. *List and index to the proceedings in Star Chamber for the reign of James I (1603-1625), in the Public Record Office, London, class*

STAC8. 3 vols. Chicago: American Bar Foundation, 1975.
- HOYLE, R. W., & SUMMERSON, H. R. T. *A handlist of Star Chamber pleadings before 1558 for Northern England.* List & Index Society, **299**. 2003.

A number of record societies have published records from Star Chamber. For details of its proceedings relating to one family, see:

- WARNEFORD, F. E., ed. *Star Chamber suits of John and Thomas Warneford,* Wiltshire Record Society, **48**. 1993.

Kings Bench

- King's Bench: records of the court c. 1200-1600
  www.nationalarchives.gov.uk/records/research-guides/kings-bench-1200-1600.htm
- King's Bench (Crown side) 1675-1875
  www.nationalarchives.gov.uk/records/research-guides/kings-bench.htm
- MEEKINGS, C. A. F. 'King's Bench Files', in BAKER, J. H., ed. *Legal records and the historian*, Royal Historical Society, 1978, pp.97-139.

The Manor of Anick-Grange } The special Court Baron of Thomas Richard Beaumont Esquire and Diana his
with the Members in the } Wife Lord and Lady of the said Manor holden there Fourth day of October in
County of Northumberland } the Year of our Lord 1810 before John Bell Gentleman, Steward of the same Court

The Names of the Jurors at the same Court.

Richard Poppin		William Lyon		William Mole	
John Dodd, Tanner	sworn.	Thomas Harrison	sworn.	John Little	sworn.
Thomas Dobson		James Garland		Thomas Yarrow	
Richard Bulman		Mathew Lee		Edward Nicholson	

At this Court came Martha Shaftoe of Hexham Widow and Relict and a Devisee named in and
by the last Will and Testament of Charles Shaftoe late of the same place Gentleman deceased, and the
Reverend Robert Clarke of Walwick Clerk and Martha his Wife Daughter and a Devisee in Tail named in and
by the said last Will and Testament of the said Charles Shaftoe deceased (She the said Martha Clarke
being first sole and secretly examined) and according to their several and respective Estates and Interests
surrendred into the Hands of the Lord and Lady of the said Manor by their Steward aforesaid One
Messuage or Stone house and a Garth or Garden with their Appurtenances situate and being in the Town
of Hexham aforesaid in a Street there called Gilligate bounding on the Burgage late of Robert
Renwick and now belonging to William Bell on the West, the Townhaugh on the North the Burgage
late of Christopher Bell and now belonging to Thomas Ramsay on the East and the Kings Street on
the South of the yearly Rent of Five Shillings and eightpence And all that Dwellinghouse and
the Garden behind the same with the Appurtenances situate standing and being in a Street of Hexham
called Hencoats and in a place there called Battle-Hill late in the Possession of the said Charles
Shaftoe and now in the Possession of the said Martha Shaftoe together with the Yard Stable and
other Buildings now held and enjoyed therewith And also the several Rooms and Closets above the
Gateway or Entry on the East side of the said House late in the Possession of the said Charles Shaftoe
and now in the Possession of the said Martha Shaftoe
together with an undivided Moiety or Half Part of and Liberty and Right of Passage at all times
hereafter through the said Gateway or Entry which said Premisses bounder on the House and
Garden formerly occupied by William Hunter and now or late belonging to Nicholas Huddock on the
East the House and Garden late belonging to William Kirsopp and now to James Kirsopp on the West
the Kings Street on the North and the Grounds called Gap Riggs on the South of the yearly Rent of
three Shillings and fourpence To the use and behoof of John Huddock of Hexham aforesaid Gentleman
his Heirs and Assigns To whom the said Lord and Lady of the Manor by their Steward aforesaid granted
Seisin of the said Premisses To have and to hold to him and to his Heirs and Assigns for ever according
to the Custom of the said Manor to the Intent and purpose only that a good and perfect Common
Recovery according to the Custom of the said Manor may be had and suffered of the said Premisses
Rendring therefore yearly to the said Lord and Lady of the Manor and to the Heirs of the said Lady
Nine Shillings at Feasts accustomed and doing other Services therefore due and of Right used Having
given to the said Lord and Lady of the Manor for his Fine and Entry, as appears in the Margin and so
forth he is thereupon admitted Tenant ——

This is a true Copy agreeing with the Records of
the Court examined by me Jno Bell Clerk

11. Anick Grange Court Baron.

CHAPTER SEVEN

Personal Records of the Gentry:
Letters, Diaries, Journals, etc.

The gentry wrote many letters, and frequently kept diaries, journals, and other personal memoranda. Letters can be found in most family archive collections. Diaries and journals frequently survive as well. These documents record the private or semi-private thoughts of your gentle ancestors; you may be able to discover much more information about your family history through these sources than by any other means. Diaries are likely to record dates of births, marriages and deaths, together with the comings and goings of relatives and friends, and much personal information. Love affairs, negotiations for marriage settlements and family settlements, estate and other business matters, political activity, church affairs - all may be discussed in these sources.

Many collections of letters have been published; some are available online. For the fifteenth century, the Paston letters reveal the hazards of gentry life in an age of constant warfare and litigation. They can be read at:

- Paston Letters (1422-1509)
  www.luminarium.org/medlit/paston.htm

Many other collections of family letters are available in print. See, for example:

- SCHOFIELD, BERTRAM, ed. *The Knyvett letters, 1620-1644.* Norfolk Record Society **20**. 1949.
- SEARLE, ARTHUR, ed. *Barrington family letters 1628-1632.* Camden 4th series **28**. Royal Historical Society, 1983.

Many diaries are also in print. One of the most famous was written by Samuel Pepys, who occupied a senior position at the Admiralty. It contains much tittle tattle about London society, and about his quarrels with his wife, as well as being an important source of information on the history of the Navy. The diary, together with many letters, has been transcribed at:

- The Diary of Samuel Pepys
  www.pepysdiary.com

12. Samuel Pepys philandering with Lady Batten, painted by J. D.Wingfield in 1861. (Wikimedia).

The Pastons and Pepys are well-known, but thousands of other diaries can be found in record offices, and many of them have been printed. Published diaries are listed by:

- MATTHEWS, W. *British diaries: an annotated bibliography of British diaries written between 1442 and 1942.* University of California Press, 1950. This is complemented by:
- HAVLICE, P. P. *And so to bed: a bibliography of diaries published in English.* Scarecrow Press, 1987.

For manuscript diaries, consult:

- BATTS, JOHN STUART. *British manuscript diaries of the 19th century: an annotated listing.* Centaur Press, 1976.

Other useful diary bibliographies include:

- GARD, R. *The observant traveller: diaries of travel in England, Wales and Scotland in the county record offices of England and Wales.* HMSO for the Association of County Archivists, 1989.
- HUFF, C. *British women's diaries: a descriptive bibliography of selected nineteenth-century women's manuscript diaries.* AIMS Press, 1985.
- CREATON, HEATHER. *Victorian diaries: the daily lives of Victorian men and women.* Mitchell Beazley, 2001.

Many gentlemen prepared guidance manuals for their heirs to use when they inherited their estates. The fortunes of a gentry family depended primarily upon its head: the wife was subordinate to him, and the children (even in adulthood) were dependent upon the will of both father and mother. Many fathers therefore thought it useful to provide their heirs with advice memoranda which summarised the lessons they had learnt from hard experience. These memoranda embodied the wisdom which the older generation thought that the younger generation would need in order to effectively defend their family's interests. Frequently they began with religious principles, whether puritan, Roman Catholic, or main-stream protestant. Most heirs were urged to energetically defend the material interests of their family; to manage their estates wisely, to be cautious but generous in their relationships with kin, tenants, and friends; to marry a wife who was not only wealthy but also virtuous. The puritan William Martyn, recorder of Exeter, expanded this advice by telling his son that 'none must be idle but every man must diligently imploy himselfe in such affaires and business as God (his master) hath committed to his care'[133]. These 'advices' can frequently be found amongst family papers in record offices; they can sometimes tell us much about a family and its attitudes.

COUNTY of *Cornwall*　　PARISH of *Advent*

Hund.ᵈ of Lesnewth

An Assessment made in Pursuance of an Act of Parliament passed in the 38th Year of His Majesty's Reign, for granting an Aid to His Majesty by a Land Tax to be raised in Great Britain, for the Service of the Year 1798.

308

No. of Register.	Names of Proprietors.	Names of Occupiers.	Sums Assessed.			Date of Contract.
			£.	s.	d.	
	M. Luxmore	Abᵐ Pethick	2	17	4	
	Dᵒ	Wᵐ Burt	2	17	4	
	Rᵗ Gwating Esq	Wᵐ Orchard	5	14	0	
	Jⁿᵒ Phil Carpenter	Thoˢ Pethick	1	14	8	
	Dᵒ	Thoˢ Joy	3	16	4	
	Dᵒ	Luscot	—	—	—	
	Thoˢ Pethick	Geo. Isbel	—	19	4	
	J. P. Carpenter Esq	Rᶜ Martin	4	10	8	
	Philip Lott	Himself	1	4	3	
	Dᵒ	Dᵒ	—	5	4¾	
	Dᵒ	Dᵒ	—	3	6	
	Jos. Stacey	Jⁿᵒ Browning	—	1	2	
	Dᵒ	Dᵒ	—	2	6	
	Dᵒ	Dᵒ	—	—	11	
	Dᵒ	Dᵒ	—	3	10	
	Dᵒ	Dᵒ	—	5	—	
	Dᵒ	Dᵒ	—	4	6	
	Dᵒ	Dᵒ	—	5	6	
	Wᵐ Burt	Himself	—	2	5	
	Dᵒ	Dᵒ	—	4	1	
	Dᵒ	Dᵒ	—	13	2	
	Ann Sloggot	Jⁿᵒ Martin	3	16	—	
	Dᵒ	Dᵒ	2	5	8	
	Thoˢ Burt	Himself	2	5	—	

13. Land Tax Redemption 1798, Advent (Cornwall). SoG Library.

CHAPTER EIGHT
Financing the Government:
Taxation and other Impositions

A. Introduction

One of the major differences between English and continental gentry was that the former had no exemption from taxation. They, like everyone else, were required to pay subsidies, hearth tax, land tax, and a range of other duties. Indeed, some impositions specifically targeted them. Until 1646, the Crown had the right to the wardship and marriage of the heirs of tenants in chief, and siphoned off the profits of large estates during minorities. After the Reformation, Roman Catholic gentry suffered from recusancy fines, which were sometimes seen as a form of taxation. Rather more seriously, gentry who fought for the Crown during the Civil War had to pay huge sums to the Parliamentary regime to 'compound for their delinquency'. The gentry frequently had no legal defence against the exactions of Crown or Protectorate.

There were a number of other government imposts on the gentry which were not, strictly speaking, direct taxation, but which nevertheless raised considerable revenue from individuals, and created extensive records which can be exploited by family historians. Some of these were ancient feudal rights of the Crown; others arose from the government's policies towards its opponents.

Records of many of these duties were made, and may now be found in record offices. They provide a huge amount of information for family and local historians.

B. Taxation

There are more ways to evade taxation than exercising a legal privilege. Despite the absence of such privilege, the gentry did not always pay their fair share of taxation. Tax was a thing to be evaded or avoided if possible.

Subsidy assessments were notoriously inaccurate; indeed, evasion of the subsidy resulted in ever decreasing yields. Parliament assigned responsibility for assessment to the gentry, who naturally sought to keep their own liability low. Even Lord Burleigh, Elizabeth's Lord Treasurer, was only assessed at £133 6s. 8d., when we know that he had an income of c.£4000 p.a. That fact did not stop him grumbling about tax dodgers in Parliament[134]. James Colbrand, a Sussex JP, argued that 'the rich were often rated ... much too low, at not a fortieth part of their wealth'[135]. On a number of occasions the subsidy was replaced by a poll tax, which was much more difficult to evade.

The Civil War resulted in the level of taxation rocketing, despite the abolition of feudal tenures. After the Restoration, the Crown demanded some recompense for its lost feudal revenues, and in 1662 the subsidy was replaced by the hearth tax. The latter received much opposition, especially in view of the fact that its collectors had to enter houses in order to check the number of hearths in them. William of Orange, when he succeeded in his bid for the English throne, sought support by abolishing the hated tax. However, he still needed money to fight his wars, a need which led him to ask Parliament to legislate for a tax on land - which lasted until the middle of the twentieth century.

Over the centuries, there have been a wide variety of other taxes imposed by government. A detailed and comprehensive list of these prior to 1688, together with information about surviving records, is provided by:

- JURKOWSKI, M., SMITH, C. L., AND CROOK, D. *Lay Taxes in England and Wales, 1188-1688.* PRO Publications, 1998.

For Tudor records, see:

- HOYLE, R. W. *Tudor taxation records: a guide for users.* PRO Publications, 1994.

Records held by TNA are described in:

- Taxation Records before 1689
  www.nationalarchives.gov.uk/records/research-guides/taxation-before-1689.htm

Taxation is the bureaucrat's delight. Assessment consumed much paper and parchment. Those taxes which have already been mentioned demanded the compilation of myriad lists of taxpayers. Some of these effectively provide lists of all householders in a parish; others are much briefer, but are still likely to mention all the gentry who lived in a particular place. Most lists for particular places commence with the leading gentry families, and may give useful information about them. Hearth tax returns, for example, are likely to reveal how many hearths there were in each household.

The majority of tax lists from the thirteenth to the seventeenth centuries are held by TNA, in class E179, and are comprehensively listed in:

- E179 Database
  www.nationalarchives.gov.uk/e179

This database enables you to identify all the tax lists in this class by place. It does not, however, index personal names. For those, it is usually necessary to consult individual documents at TNA. However, many have been published by record societies and others. See, for example:

- ERSKINE, A. M., ed. *The Devon lay subsidy of 1323*. Devon & Cornwall Record Society new series **14**. 1969.
- HOYLE, R., ed. *Early Tudor Craven: subsidies and assessments, 1510-1547*. Yorkshire Archaeological Society record series **145**. 1987.

The British Record Society **www.britishrecordsociety.org** is currently seeking to ensure that there is at least one published hearth tax return for each English county. A full listing of published hearth tax returns can be found at:

- Roehampton University Centre for Hearth Tax Research: Bibliography
  www.roehampton.ac.uk/hearthtax/publications/Hearth%20Tax%20Bibliography/index.html

Full lists of published returns of both the subsidy and the hearth tax, and of other taxes, are given in the present author's series of county bibliographies, as well as in the books by Jurkowski, et al, and Hoyle, listed above.

The subsidy was only to be paid once. Where taxpayers were liable to assesment in more than one hundred - which was the case for many gentry - they could obtain a certificate of residence from the subsidy commissioner whom they had paid. These could be produced to the commissioner(s) for any other hundred(s) where the taxpayer was liable to be assessed. Many of these certificates are now in TNA. Some are in class E179, but most are in E115. The latter are now listed by name in TNA's catalogue.

The land tax was levied from 1692. Returns list the names of landowners and, in theory, their tenants. Unfortunately, many returns have been lost. Most of those which remain owe their survival to the fact that payment of tax on land worth £2 or more provided evidence of entitlement to vote. The majority of surviving returns dated from c.1780 to c.1832, and are to be found in local record offices. TNA does hold a full set of returns for 1798, in class IR23. These returns have been digitised at:

* UK Land Tax Redemption 1798
  http://search.ancestry.co.uk/search/db.aspx?dbid=2319

A full listing of surviving returns is provided by:

* GIBSON, JEREMY, MEDLYCOTT, MERVYN, & MILLS, DENNIS. *Land and window tax assessments.* 2nd ed. Federation of Family History Societies, 1998 (2004 reprint).

For a detailed guide, see:

* UNWIN, R. W. *Search guide to the English land tax.* West Yorkshire County Record Office, 1992.

A legacy duty was briefly imposed in 1780, but it was not until 1796 that death duties became permanent. At first, they were confined to no more than 25% of estates, but by 1857 they were levied on all estates worth more than £20. Registers are available in TNA (Class IR26, with annual indexes in IR27) for the period 1796-1903. Much of the information in these registers was based on wills, the dates of which are noted, together with the date of probate and the names of the executors. The registers record names of the deceased, with their addresses, occupations, and dates of death. Details of the value of the estate, legacies, and the duty paid are also noted, as are details of legatees and next of kin. Annotations on the registers could be made many years after they had been compiled, and may note details of spouse's deaths, the marriages and deaths of legatees, and changes of their addresses. A variety of other information may also be given.

Researchers should consult the TNA research guide for further information:

• Death duty records 1796 to 1903
  www.nationalarchives.gov.uk/records/research-guides/death-duty-records-1796-to-1903.htm

An online pay-per-view index to the registers is available. This is effectively also an index to all wills which attracted death duty. See:

• Search the Index to Death Duty registers 1796-1903
  www.findmypast.co.uk/DeathDutyStartSearchServlet

See also:

• *Inland Revenue Estate Duty registers and indexes (IR26, IR27), 1796-1894.* List & Index Society, **177**. 1981.

The gentry were also subject to a variety of other levies. These included duties on armorial bearings (1793-1830), carriages (from 1747-1782), silver plate (1756-1777), saddle and carriage horses (1784-1830), racing horses (from 1784), men servants (1777-1789), women servants (1785-1791), dogs (1796-1830), and clocks and watches (1797-1798). From 1797, these 'assessed taxes' were collected together. Parish assessments are in TNA, class E182, some with names. Some information can also be found in E181.

Wiltshiremen who paid the hair powder duty in 1796 and 1797 are listed in:

• HURLEY, BERYL, ed. *The hair powder tax, 1796 and 1797, Wiltshire.* Wiltshire Family History Society, 1997.

A list of those assessed to the male servants duty for 1780 can be found in TNA, class T47/8. An index to the employers (mostly gentry) in this list is held by the Society of Genealogists. Some records can also be found in local record offices.

Annual lists of those who paid silver plate duty between 1756 and 1768 are in TNA, class T47/4-5; lists of actual and suspected defaulters are in T47/6-7. Those who paid carriage duty between 1753 and 1766 are listed in T47/2-5.

C. Forced Loans

When Tudor and Stuart governments needed money, but did not wish to ask Parliament to vote a subsidy, they sometimes compelled their subjects to make a forced loan. Records of forced loans can be found amongst the records of various other taxes in TNA, class E179[136].

Forced loans were a particular characteristic of Henry VIII's and Charles I's governments, although all of the Tudors and the early Stuarts levied them. In 1522, they were associated with military musters. The 1522 returns give much more information than merely men and equipment; they also listed all landowners, and valued their lands. They also listed all males over 16, and valued their goods. For a list of returns, see:

- CORNWALL, J. 'A Tudor Domesday: The Musters of 1522', *Journal of the Society of Archivists*, **3**(1), 1965, pp.19-24.

Some records are in print. See, for example:

- CORNWALL, JULIAN, ed. *Tudor Rutland: The County Community under Henry VIII.* Rutland Record Series **1**. 1980.
- FARADAY, MICHAEL A., ed. *Worcestershire taxes in the 1520s: the military survey and forced loans of 1522-1523 and the lay subsidy of 1524-1527.* Worcestershire Historical Society, new series **19**. 2003.

The forced loans imposed by Charles I were a major contributory factor to his conflict with Parliament, and helped set the scene for the Civil War. Sources for his levies are discussed in:

- CUST, RICHARD. 'A list of commissioners for the forced loan of 1626-1627', *Bulletin of the Institute of Historical Research* **51**(124), 1978, pp.199-206. (No names are given).

The activities of Caroline royal commissioners were surpassed by their immediate successors under the Long Parliament. The Committee for the Advance of Money was established in order to demand loans 'on the public faith'. In 1643, a contribution of one twentieth of real, and one fifth of personal estate was demanded. If payment was refused, goods and lands could be seized. £260,306 14s. 5d. had been received by 1 July 1644. Nevertheless, payment in full was rare, and could not be enforced in areas under Royalist control.

Only those with property worth more than £100 were liable to pay. Most payers were therefore gentry. The proceedings of the Committee provide much interesting information on gentry assessments. For example, it imprisoned Margaret Garway in 'Peter House' for her failure to pay her assessment of £150 - but granted her leave to visit her pregnant daughter during her confinement.

The proceedings of the Committee have been partially calendared:

* GREEN, MARY ANNE EVERETT, ed. *Calendar of the proceedings of the Committee for Advance of Money, 1642-1656.* 3 vols. H.M.S.O., 1888. There is a digitised version at **http://www.british-history.ac.uk/catalogue.aspx?type=3&gid=111**

Microfilm of the original documents are included in the Harvester microfilm edition of state papers[137].

D. Inquisitions Post Mortem

In feudal theory, all land was held from the Crown, who originally had the right to demand military service from landowners who held their property directly from the King (tenants in chief). Such land was held by knight service. When a tenant in chief died, his land escheated to the Crown. His heir was required to pay a relief to the Crown on taking possession; if he was under age, the Crown had the right to the revenue of his estate until he came of age, and could also select the heir's bride. By the fifteenth century, the basis of the feudal system, i.e. the obligation of military service in return for land, had withered away. The tenants in chief had ceased to have the prime responsibility for serving the crown[138]. The Crown's need for money, however, was ever increasing, and the government steadily increased its demands for feudal incidents such as wardship and marriage[139]. At the beginning of Edward VI's reign, income from wardships and marriages averaged £1117 per annum; when Charles I's Court ceased functioning in the 1640s, the average was £39,819 per annum[140]. The Crown was supposed to 'live of its own', without the need for Parliamentary grants of taxation. Feudal incidents were 'its own'. Henry VII began the practice of conducting vigorous inquiries into the lands of deceased tenants in chief. He also issued many commissions to investigate 'concealments'. The latter may be found in the patent rolls[141].

In practice, wardships and marriages were sold to the highest bidder. The committee, as the purchaser was known, did not necessarily have any connection with the ward's family. Out of 232 wardships granted under Edward VI, only 46 went to the mother, other kin, or the ward himself. The proportion of grants to kin steadily increased; after

1611, it was the Crown's deliberate policy to prefer kin as committees. In 1628-1630, 128 out of 222 wardships went to kin[142]. But the Crown also began to demand higher fines from committees, based on more accurate assessments of the value of the estate. A minority could be expensive for a gentle family: the Portmans of Somerset had to pay £2300 in 1612, and another £1800 in 1621[143]. In 1612, Christopher Wandesford of Kirklington (Yorkshire) was the fifth successive heir to inherit as a minor; his daughter thought that the financial consequences of wardship had reduced the family estate to a quarter or a fifth of what it had once been[144]. Much money also had to be laid out on the fees of officers of the Court of Wards. The purchaser had responsibility for the administration of the estate, as well as the care, education, and marriage of the ward (at least until he came of age). The process of wardship was administered by the Court of Wards and Liveries from 1540. Wardship and other feudal duties were abolished in 1646.

The Crown appointed escheators in each county[145] who were required to conduct inquisitions, before a jury, into the properties of deceased tenants in chief. This was the essential preliminary before lands could descend to heirs. The resultant *inquisitions post mortem* give details of the lands held, of whom they were held and their tenure, the date of death, and the name of the heir. These documents are now held in TNA, amongst the records of the Chancery (C132), the Exchequer (E149), and the Court of Wards (WARD7). The Palatine counties of Cheshire and Lancashire, and the Duchy of Lancaster, were administered separately; their inquisitions are in CHES3, DURH3, PL4 and DL7. For more information on these documents, consult:

- Inquisitions post mortem, Henry III-Charles I: landholders and heirs
  www.nationalarchives.gov.uk/records/research-guides/inqusitions-post-mortem.htm

See also (especially for printed indexes and calendars):

- Public Records: Inquisitions Post Mortem
  www.medievalgenealogy.org.uk/guide/ipm.shtml

A calendar of *inquisitions post mortem* (begun in 1904) is currently in progress:

- *Calendar of inquisitions post mortem and other analogous documents preserved in the Public Record Office.* HMSO, 1904- . To be continued. 1st series (26 vols, to date) covers 1235-1447; 2nd series (3 vols) covers 1485-1509.

Fifteenth century *inquisitions post mortem* are listed and indexed in:

- *Lists of Inquisitions post mortem, Henry V-Richard III; Inquisitions ad quod damnum and miscellaneous inquisitions, Henry VII-Charles I (C138-C142).* List & Index Society **268**. 1998.
- *Name index to Chancery Inquisitions post mortem, Henry V-Richard III (C 138-C142).* List & Index Society **269**. 1998.

More recent *inquisitions post mortem* can be found through TNA's online catalogue. For a full printed index, 1509-1646, see:

- *Index of inquisitions preserved in the Public Record Office.* Lists and Indexes **23**, **26**, **31** and **33**. Amended ed. Kraus Reprint, 1963. Contents Vol.1. Henry VIII to Philip & Mary. Vol.2. Elizabeth. Vol.3. James I. Vol.4. Charles I and later. The reprint is to be preferred to the original edition, since it incorporates many mss additions to that edition.

A number of record societies have published edited versions of inquisitions post mortem for particular counties. See, for example:

- *Abstracts of Wiltshire inquisitions post mortem returned into the Court of Chancery in the reign of King Charles the First.* Index Library **23**. British Record Society / Wiltshire Archaeological & Natural History Society, 1901.

The Court of Wards had two other records to help it determine fines. Purchasers had to submit 'confessions' of the value of each estate. These confessions included notes on encumbrances such as debts, legacies, jointures, etc. There are also the feodaries' certificates of the value of each estate. Feodaries were present whenever an inquisition was held, and held a watching brief for the Court of Wards. Their surveys usually place a higher value on lands than do *inquisitions post mortem,* although valuations may still be lower than actual values. Sir Thomas Wentworth held the opinion that even the feodaries frequently under-valued lands. But he also thought that if valuations in *inquisitions post mortem* were increased to realistic levels there would be a 'mighty noise'[146].

A variety of other documents can also be found amongst the Court's records: pleadings, depositions, deeds, extents, *etc.* All these can be found in TNA, in a variety of different WARD classes (which are not arranged systematically). For example, WARD 2 includes numerous deeds and evidences exhibited in case heard before the court, and not subsequently returned to their owners. These are searchable in TNA's catalogue.

For the records of the Court of Wards, see:

* Court of Wards and Liveries: land inheritance 1540-1645
  www.nationalarchives.gov.uk/records/research-guides/wards-and-liveries.htm

Useful histories of the Court are provided by:

* BELL, H. E. *An introduction to the history and records of the Court of Wards and Liveries.* Cambridge University Press, 1953.
* HURSTFIELD, JOEL. *The Queen's wards: wardship and marriage under Elizabeth I.* Longmans Green & Co., 1958.

A collection of documents from the Court is edited in:

* HAWKINS, M. J., ed. *Sales of wards in Somerset, 1603-1641.* Somerset Record Society, **67**. 1965.

E. Compositions for Knighthood

One of the expedients adopted by Charles I to raise money was to enforce legislation of the reign of Edward II relating to knighthood. This legislation required everyone who possessed lands worth over £40 per annum to attend at the King's coronation in order to receive the degree of knighthood. Those who had failed to do so were required to pay 'compositions' for their failure. Sampson Hele, a wealthy Devon JP, had to pay no less than £150 in 1633[147]. The instructions to the Composition Commissioners specified that no JP should be allowed to pay less than £25, 'it beinge presumed that they are all of good estates'[148]. Records of those who paid can be found in TNA, E407/35 and E178. Some lists have been published in local journals; see, for example:

* FRY, E. A. 'Knighthood compositions for Dorset', *Notes & queries for Somerset & Dorset* **4**, 1894-1895, pp.14-21.
* ELLIS, SIR HENRY. 'Compositions for knighthood, temp Charles I', *Sussex archaeological collections* **16**, 1864, pp.45-51.

F. Recusancy Fines

Another source of income for the government were the fines imposed on those who refused to attend Church of England services after 1559. These recusants, initially, were mostly Roman Catholics, although a few were more extreme puritans[149]. The survival of Roman Catholicism depended upon the support of the gentry, and Roman Catholic missionary priests tended to itinerate between gentlemen's houses.

In 1559, the Elizabethan regime imposed a penalty of 1/- for each absence from church. The perceived threat from Papists steadily increased during the course of the reign. So did the penalties. They were increased to £20 per month in 1581. Subsequent legislation authorised the forfeiture of all goods owned, and of two-thirds of real property.

Fines were originally collected by churchwardens, and appear in their accounts. When recusancy was made an indictable offence in 1581, the responsibility for levying fines was transferred to Quarter Sessions. Its records therefore include details of recusants. From 1591, the greater severity resulting from the Spanish Armada led to the compilation of annual recusant rolls, listing fines imposed in each county. These were sent up to London, and enabled the government to obtain an overall picture of the extent of recusancy. They are now in TNA, class E376 and E377. Many have been published by the Catholic Record Society **www.catholic-history.org.uk/crs.** See, for example:

- BOWLER, HUGH, ed. *Recusant roll no.2 (1593-1594).* Catholic Record Society **57.** 1965.

Roman Catholics were not only liable to fines for failure to attend church. There were a range of other penalties. Subsidy assessments, for example, were doubled. They could be fined for harbouring other recusants, for refusing to take communion, for sending their sons overseas to study at Catholic institutions.

For most recusants, the penalties imposed, although high, were not ruinous. Despite their Catholicism, and even despite the execution of one of its members for plotting against Queen Elizabeth in 1583, the Throckmorton family managed to hold on to its estate at Coughton (Warwickshire) throughout the penal years, and are still there today[150]. Fines were frequently regarded as a form of taxation, rather than as a penalty for illegality - a fact which was deplored by the Long Parliament[151]. The fine of £20 per month was not usually levied regularly or consistently. Indeed, there were only 13 families in the whole country who were compelled to pay in full for extended periods of time[152]. Many estates escaped seizure by the use of fraudulent conveyances, on technicalities, or with the connivance of Crown officers. Those estates which were seized were frequently drastically under-valued by local officials and jurors. The Crown barely received £40 from the lands of the Vavasours, which were worth £2000 per annum[153]. A handful did suffer severely. Francis Tregian[154] spent many years in prison for harbouring a Catholic priest, Cuthbert Mayne (who was executed). But even the £7720 in fines and other penalties imposed upon Sir Thomas Tresham[155] between 1581 and 1605 did not ruin him, and must be set against the fact that he paid £12,000 for his six daughters' marriage portions.

The consequence of the penalties imposed on Catholic gentry was that they tended to become a class within a class. As the dividing line between Catholic and Protestant became ever more strongly defined, and as the number of Catholics decreased, the 'Papists' increasingly became a tightly-knit group of families with their own priests, their own system of education, their own lawyers specialising in recusancy work, and even their own Catholic physicians. There was frequent inter-marriage within this group, who regularly met together to dine, to hunt, or to worship[156].

Anti-Catholic legislation was not repealed until the nineteenth century. Nevertheless, after the Restoration, the recusancy laws were more observed in the breach than in the observance. Fines were rarely levied, and very little land was forfeited, except after the 1715 and 1745 rebellions. Nevertheless, recusants liable to the land tax theoretically had to pay double the amount of their normal assessment. This was sometimes a heavy burden, especially in periods when the rate of tax was high. Full payment, however, could frequently be evaded or avoided. Even if the Crown had had the will to fully enforce penal legislation, it did not have the efficient and reliable bureaucracy that would have enabled it to do so. It was easy for a recusant family such as the Pudseys to evade the law. Thomas Pudsey grew wealthy by specialising in recusancy law; he used many stratagems to deflect the attention of the authorities from his own recusancy. For example, when he bought the manor of Hackforth (Yorkshire) he conveyed it to nominees who lived in Southern England, for their own use - although in practice he took the profits. When the churchwardens sought to indict him for recusancy, he managed to persuade them to indict only his wife - under a false name, so that when process issued out of the Exchequer no fine could be levied[157].

A wide range of records relating to the fines and sufferings of Roman Catholics can be found in TNA. For a detailed guide to these records, consult:

- WILLIAM, J. ANTHONY. *Sources for recusant history (1559-1791) in English official archives.* Recusant history **16**(4), 1983.

The TNA website has two useful research guide:

- Catholics
  www.nationalarchives.gov.uk/records/research-guides/catholics.htm

- Catholic Recusants
  www.nationalarchives.gov.uk/records/research-guides/catholic-recusants.htm

See also:

- GANDY, MICHAEL. *Tracing your Catholic ancestors in England.* Basic facts about ... series. Federation of Family History Societies, 1998.

Many related publications are listed in:

- GANDY, M. *Catholic family history: a bibliography of general sources.* The Author, 1996.
- GANDY, M. *Catholic family history: a bibliography of local sources.* The Author, 1996.

G. Delinquents' Compositions

Recusants were not the only members of the gentry whose estates were liable to be seized by the government. In 1643, during the Civil War, both the King and Parliament ordered that the lands of their opponents should be seized. The lands of some Parliamentary supporters probably were seized; at least we know that Royalist sequestrators were at work in Glamorganshire in 1643[158]. Parliamentary victory meant that the records of most Royalist sequestrators were destroyed. Royalist 'delinquents', however, can be traced in the extensive archives of the Parliamentary Committee for Compounding with Delinquents and related committees, sometimes referred to as the Royalist Composition Papers.

The term 'Composition' refers to the fact that most Royalists whose estate had been seized were permitted to make a 'composition' for its return, provided that they took an oath of loyalty - the 'Solemn League & Covenant' - to Parliament. Some 3,225 'delinquents' took advantage of this provision[159]. The local Parliamentary 'County Committee' had first to make a survey of the estate, including information concerning any liabilities it had to meet. The Committeemen also reported on the extent of the delinquent's participation in the war. From this information the Parliamentary authorities determined the fine to be levied, expressed as a percentage of the value of the estate. Once half the fine was paid, the delinquent regained his use of the estate.

The process of composition was bureaucratic, and created a substantial archive. Papers relating to a particular estate can tell us much about its owner's experience of war. Col Ralph Sneyd of Keele Hall (Staffordshire) sought to compound in 1645, saying that he had been in arms against the Parliament, although, as an MP, he had not attended the Oxford Parliament. In 1646, however, he was said to be again in arms. When he was killed in 1651, his brother William was left to pay off the final £500 of his fine. The papers also reveal much information concerning Sneyd's debts, and the difficulties his creditors had in securing payment[160].

The valuations placed on compounders' estates must not be taken at face value. Under-valuation and evasion were rife, as might be expected. Many on the Parliamentary side agreed with Sir John Holland, who expressed his abhorrence of being obliged to act against those 'to whome I have the neerest relations of blood and obligations of friendship'[161]. The advice proferred by Sir Ralph Verney was followed by most Royalist gentry: 'Prepare a particular of your lands with as much art as you can, and be sure to clog it with as much debt as you can'[162]. Royalists could attempt to deny their delinquency, they could under-value or conceal their lands, they could inflate its encumbrances, they could claim that they were only life-tenants of an estate vested in trustees, they could use the influence of friends who were close to the regime. Even if their land was sold, it was often purchased by their nominees.

The penalties imposed for delinquency, like those imposed for recusancy, did not usually cause 'delinquents' to lose their lands. After the restoration, many sought compensation for their losses, and great play was made of royalist 'sufferings'. But actually only a few families completely lost their estates. Most of these had already been in financial difficulties. The Royalist gentry re-emerged after the Restoration, shaken, but mostly still in possession of their estates, and still able to control their communities.

The papers of the Committee for Compounding in class SP23 are calendared in:

- GREEN, MARY ANNE EVERETT, ed. *Calendar of the Committee for Compounding with Delinquents, &c., 1643-1660.* 5 vols. 1889-1893. They are also available on microfilm in the Harvester Press edition of the State Papers Domestic (see below, p.121)

These papers are complemented by the Sequestration Committee's books and papers. Its papers, in class SP20, are about to be catalogued by TNA.

Two TNA research guides provide useful information about the Royalist Composition Papers, together with valuable guidance concerning the records of related committees:

- State Papers Domestic: Commonwealth 1642-1660
  www.nationalarchives.gov.uk/records/research-guides/state-papers-commonwealth-1642-1660.htm

- Crown, church and royalist lands 1642-1660
  www.nationalarchives.gov.uk/records/research-guides/crown-church-royalist-lands.htm

Information may also be found amongst the papers of the Parliamentary county committees. Many records - especially accounts - of these committees can be found amongst the Commonwealth Exchequer Papers (Class SP28), which are included in the Harvester microfilm of the State Papers[163]. Some county committee order books survive in the British Library and elsewhere. For an example, which also includes extracts from SP28, see:

- PENNINGTON, D. H., & ROOTS, I. A., eds. *The Committee at Stafford 1643-1645*. Manchester University Press / Staffordshire Record Society, 1957.

H. Other Forfeitures

It was not only the Interregnum regime which enforced forfeitures of property on those who opposed its rule. Forfeiture was a frequent penalty for treason or rebellion. Many inventories of the goods of persons attainted of treason can be found in TNA, classes E154 and LR2. The reports of commissions of inquiry into their property, 1558-1901 can be found in E178.

The Forfeited Estates Commission was set up to administer the estates forfeited by the Jacobite rebels of 1715. Its records are also in TNA. FEC1 is a large collection of deeds and related documents, many dating back to the sixteenth century, produced before the Commissioners. FEC2 includes the Commissioners' minute books, together with registers of forfeited estates and of claims against them. These records (mostly from Northern England) are described in detail by:

- BARLOW, D. *The records of the Forfeited Estates Commission*. Public Record Office handbooks **12**. HMSO, 1968.

For a listing of all the names mentioned in FEC1, see:

- JOLLY, EMMA. 'Jacobite material: the records of the Forfeited Estates Commission for England', *Genealogists' Magazine* **28**(11), 2006, pp.493-498.

See also TNA's research guide:

- Jacobite Risings 1715 and 1745
  www.nationalarchives.gov.uk/records/research-guides/jacobite-risings.htm

CHAPTER NINE

Supporting the Government:
Loyalty Oaths and Poll Books

A. Loyalty Oaths

The threat of rebellion was taken very seriously by the Crown. Between 1485 and 1688, there were no less than four successful risings. Henry Tudor came to the throne after defeating Richard III at the Battle of Bosworth in 1485. His grand-daughter Mary successfully rose against the government of Lady Jane Grey. Parliament led the revolt against Charles I, which resulted in the king losing his head. And William of Orange's challenge resulted in James II fleeing the realm. The threat of revolt was not to be taken lightly.

That being so, governments endeavoured to use all the means in their power to prevent rebellion. The demand for an oath of allegiance was one means by which they sought to maintain their control. Such oaths could be used to challenge the consciences of potential rebels, and to ensure that those who were not prepared to take them were excluded from public office. Oaths were imposed *en masse* at a number of critical moments. At other times, office holders were required to demonstrate their loyalty by attending church and taking the sacrament.

The first critical moment was the outbreak of the Civil War, when the House of Commons demanded that subjects take a 'Protestation' promising to defend the Church of England, the King, and Parliament. The connection between these three elements of the constitution was so close that the House refused to acknowledge that there might be any conflict between them (despite the fact that conflict was glaringly obvious). Those who refused to take the Protestation were to be denied the right to hold any public office. Ministers, churchwardens, constables, and overseers of the poor were required to take the oath before Justices of the Peace in their local market town. They were then expected to administer it in their own parishes, and to record the names of oath-takers. Parish returns are frequently headed by the names of local gentry. If they are not present, that is good evidence that either they were recusants, or they were away from home, perhaps supporting one side or the other. Returns were sent to Westminster, and are now in the Parliamentary Archives **www.parliament.uk/ business/publications/parliamentary-archives**. Returns survive for approximately a third of English parishes. Many have been published. For full details of surviving and published returns, see:

- GIBSON, JEREMY, & DELL, ALAN. *The protestation returns and other contemporary listings*. Federation of Family History Societies, 1995 (2004 reprint).

Gibson and Dell also list the few surviving returns from the Vow and Covenant of 1643, and the Solemn League and Covenant of 1644. These oaths were probably only taken in areas controlled by Parliamentary forces. There is no central collection of returns, but they can sometimes be found amongst records from parish chests.

Another important collection of returns are those from the Association Oath of 1695-6. The attempted assassination of William III prompted Parliament to call for this oath of association, which attracted the signatures of most gentry and office holders. The oath rolls are now in TNA, class C213 and KB24. Some have been published; see, for example:

- GANDY, WALLACE, ed. 'The Association Oath rolls for Buckinghamshire, A.D.1696', *Records of Buckinghamshire,* **11**, 1920-1926, pp.109-120. This is now available online: **www.bucksas.org.uk/rob/rob_11_3_109.pdf**
- GANDY, WALLACE, ed. *The Lancashire Association Oath rolls, A.D. 1696.* Society of Genealogists, 1921. Reprinted 1985.
- WEBB, CLIFF. *Association Oath Rolls for Surrey 1695.* 1 fiche in folder. West Surrey Family History Society, [198-]. These Surrey rolls, together with those for London livery companies, are available on British Origins at:
- About Association Oath Rolls
  www.origins.net/help/aboutbo-aor.aspx

For a full listing of surviving rolls in class C213, see:

- WEBB, C. R. 'The Association Oath Rolls of 1695', *Genealogists' Magazine* **21**(4), 1983, pp.120-23.

Oaths were not just demanded in times of crisis. The Restoration government of Charles II sought to exclude all Roman Catholics and dissenters from holding any public office. It did this by insisting that office holders had to receive holy communion from a Church of England clergyman. This requirement was first enforced on elected officers of Corporations by the Corporation Act 1661. It was extended to all office holders by the Test Act 1672. In 1702, a further requirement was added; office holders had to swear to deny the right of James II's exiled son to the throne.

Sacrament certificates give details of where and when Holy Communion was taken, together with the names of the clergyman, churchwarden, and two witnesses. They can be found amongst the records of Quarter Sessions. Many are also held by TNA, in a variety of different classes. Most of the latter relate to the area within 30 miles of the metropolis. Full details of TNA holdings are given in:

- Oath Rolls and Sacrament Certificates after 1660
  www.nationalarchives.gov.uk/records/research-guides/oath-rolls.htm

Details of sacrament certificates from the Isle of Wight are presented in:

- Isle of Wight Council: Sacrament Certificates 1673-1827
  http://iwight.com/RecOffice_DBs/sacraments.aspx

B. Poll Books

Loyalty oaths were not the only means of maintaining the security of the realm. Parliaments were also important. They were supposed to ensure that the gentry, and, through them, the rest of the community, provided the support needed by the crown. That, at least, was the theory, although it did not quite work in the mid-seventeenth century. It was not until the Crown accepted the dominant role of Parliament after the Glorious Revolution that theory became practice.

The House of Commons was elected by freeholders in the counties, and by a variety of different electors in the boroughs - each borough had its own franchise, some of which were very small. We will see in the next chapter how the gentry served as MPs for many boroughs, as well as for the counties. Here, we are concerned with the gentry as electors.

In the counties, the franchise was held by everyone who possessed freehold land worth more than 40/- per annum. This level had been set in 1429, when it had excluded all but the gentry. They continued to be the most influential people in county electorates until the nineteenth century.

From 1696, the sheriff as returning officer was required to compile lists of everyone who voted, showing how they cast their votes. These poll books, as they are called, frequently give information such as abode and occupation. County poll books enable the genealogist to identify where the gentry voted, and how they used their influence.

Some poll books were printed, others are still in manuscript. Most local studies collections and/or record offices hold collections for their own areas. There are particularly good collections at the Institute of Historical Research, the British Library, and the Society of Genealogists. Many of those at the Society of Genealogists have been digitised and are available for members to view at **www.sog.org.uk**.

Between c1780 and 1832, poll books can be used in conjunction with Land Tax returns[164], which were used to determine who was eligible to vote. From 1832, this use of the land tax returns was discontinued; instead, separate electoral registers were compiled. Detailed listings of poll books and electoral registers are available in the Gibson guides series:

- GIBSON, JEREMY, & ROGERS, COLIN. *Poll books 1696-1872: a directory to holdings in Great Britain.* 4th ed. Family History Partnership, 2008.
- GIBSON, JEREMY. *Electoral registers 1832-1948; and burgess rolls.* Family History Partnership, 2008.

C. Jurors' Lists

Most gentlemen were liable to serve on juries, albeit many jurors would have been minor gentry rather than the elite. The qualification for jury service, under an act of 1692, was possession of lands worth more than £6 per annum. Jurors had to be aged between 21 and 70. From 1696, parish constables were required to compile annual lists of the names and residences of everyone qualified to serve, and to return it to Quarter Sessions. These lists were copied into books, and a duplicate was given to the sheriff. These lists are sometimes referred to as freeholders' lists, and can be found amongst Quarter Sessions records.

CHAPTER TEN

The Gentry as a Ruling Class: Members of Parliament, Sheriffs, Justices of the Peace, etc.

A. Introduction

The gentry, it was pointed out in chapter 1, were the workhorses of local government. Their ancestors had responded to the widening exercise of royal justice in the late thirteenth century by harnessing it to their own purposes, and by taking the offices which the Crown created for themselves. As Justices of the Peace and sheriffs, they governed the shires. As bureaucrats, they organized the collection of taxes[165]. As deputy lieutenants, they organised the county militia. As representatives of the community they served as Members of Parliament, and acted as conduits between the Crown and its subjects. They thus laid the foundation of gentry dominance in local government[166].

These activities were all dependent upon what has been called the territoriality of the gentry[167], the link between the gentry and their localities. Gentlemen were at the top of the social pile in their local communities; their offices served to accentuate the social difference between themselves and the people they governed. Office holding also created that sense of community and exclusiveness within the landed classes that was maintained until the twentieth century.

The offices which the gentry held created many records, which are now available for researchers. Members of Parliament are particularly well documented, but Justices of the Peace, sheriffs, and various other officers have also left paper trails that can reveal a great deal about their activities.

B. Members of Parliament

Most MPs were gentlemen. If they could, candidates sought to represent county constituencies, rather than the boroughs. In practice, however, most of the boroughs elected gentlemen rather than their own burgesses to represent them. The gentry demanded seats, and had the influence to ensure that they won them. At Cirencester in the eighteenth century, if members of the Bathurst or Master families sought election, they were sure to be elected[168]. Few merchants or other tradesmen sat in Parliament. William Stumpe, the clothier, did sit for Malmesbury in the Reformation Parliament, but after the accession of Queen Elizabeth, he had very few successors: the last instance of a clothier representing a Wiltshire borough was when John Noyes was elected for Calne in the first Parliament of James I[169].

Membership of Parliament was viewed by the gentry in a variety of different ways. Some saw membership as denoting their status in county society. Others saw it as a duty that they were obliged to perform. Still others used it for personal gain, or even as a means to escape their debtors. Ralph Sneyd of Keele Hall may have become an MP in the Long Parliament in order to prevent bailiffs from arresting him for debt.

Members of Parliament have perhaps been more studied than any other occupation. A huge amount of information about them is available in print. MPs to 1874 are listed in a *Parliamentary Paper*:

- *Return of the names of every member of the lower house of the Parliaments of England Scotland and Ireland, with name of constituency represented and date of return, 1213-1874.* 3 vols. House of Commons papers 1878. LXII, pts.1-3. HMSO, 1874.

The series of biographical dictionaries published or planned by the History of Parliament Trust **www.histparl.ac.uk** will eventually provide brief but authoritative biographies for every MP from 1386 to 1868. They will also include detailed information about why people wanted to be MPs, and how they sought to achieve their aim. The works currently available are listed below, together with a number of other biographical dictionaries which fill some of the gaps.

- ROSKELL, J. S., CLARK, LINDA, & RAWCLIFFE, CAROLE, eds. *The Commons 1386-1421.* 4 vols. History of Parliament Trust, 1993.

- WEDGWOOD, JOSIAH C., & HOLT, ANNE D. *History of Parliament: biographies of the members of the Commons house, 1439-1509*. HMSO, 1936.
- BINDOFF, S. T., ed. *The Commons 1509-1558*. 3 vols. Secker & Warburg, 1982
- HASLER, P. W., ed. *The Commons 1558-1603*. 3 vols. Secker & Warburg, 1982.
- KEELER, MARY FREAR. *The Long Parliament 1640-41: a biographical study of its members*. Philadelphia: American Philosophical Society, 1954.
- HENNING, B. D., ed. *The Commons 1660-1690*. 3 vols. Secker & Warburg, 1983.
- CRUICKSHANKS, EVELINE, HANDLEY, STUART, & HAYTON, DAVID, eds. *The Commons 1690-1715*. 5 vols. Cambridge University Press, 2002.
- SEDGWICK, ROMNEY, ed. *The Commons 1715-1754*. 2 volumes. HMSO, 1971.
- NAMIER, LEWIS, SIR, & BROOKE, JOHN, eds. *The Commons 1754-1790*. 3 vols. Secker & Warburg, 1964. Reprinted HMSO, 1985.
- THORNE, R. G., ed. *The Commons 1790-1820*. 5 vols. Secker & Warburg, 1986.

For more recent MPs, see:

- STENTON, MICHAEL, et al. *Who's who of British members of parliament: a biographical dictionary of the House of Commons*. 4 vols. Harvester Press, 1976-1981. Contents: Vol.1. 1832-1885. Vol.2. 1886-1918. Vol.3. 1919-45. Vol.4. 1945-1979.

There are also many biographical dictionaries listing MPs for particular counties and boroughs. These cannot be listed here, but can be identified in the present author's county bibliographies.

C. Sheriffs

After the Norman conquest, the sheriff became the principal officer of the crown in each county, and also in county boroughs. Norman sheriffs were very powerful, and therefore much disliked. Political pressure resulted in the office becoming an annual appointment in 1258. In the fourteenth century many of the sheriff's judicial duties were transferred to Justices of the Peace. His responsibilities for the militia were transferred to Lords Lieutenant in the sixteenth century. The office became increasingly ceremonial in character, although it continued to be an expensive honour. Sheriffs even had to pay fees in order to take up their office, and to settle their accounts. They had to entertain the Assize judges, they had to ensure that taxes were collected, and they had to preside at Parliamentary elections. They were not allowed to leave the county during their year of office.

Much of the sheriff's work was done by under sheriffs, whose corruption or incompetence could lead to the sheriff facing costly litigation, or being heavily fined for negligence. The shrievalty of Sir Henry Cholmley of Whitby in 1624 is said to have cost him £1000[170]. According to Sir Simonds D'Ewes[171], the position was 'an unwelcome preferment' to many. Nevertheless, some welcomed the opportunity it presented to make or enhance their reputation. Richard Grenville was knighted for his service as sheriff; he had conducted a vigorous campaign against the Cornish Papists[172]. Serving as sheriff was a good preparation for standing for Parliament; all of Gloucestershire's seventeenth-century MPs had served as sheriff before their elections. The prestige of the office declined in the eighteenth century, and the office was frequently evaded by the landed elite. In the nineteenth century, the prestige of the office began to rise again[173].

Sheriffs were chosen from amongst the wealthiest members of the gentry; in Tudor and Stuart times most were knights or baronets. The sheriffs' rolls in TNA, classes C227 (1531-1678) and C172 (1700-1842) record the names of candidates for the office, and of those chosen. These are discussed in:

• WILSON, JEAN.S. 'Sheriffs' rolls of the 16th and 17th centuries', *English historical review* **47**, 1932, pp.31-45.

Appointments were also listed in the *London gazette* **www.london-gazette.co.uk**. A published list of sheriffs can be found in:

• *List of sheriffs for England and Wales from the earliest times to 1831, compiled from documents in the Public Record Office.* Lists and Indexes **9**. HMSO, 1896. Reprinted New York: Kraus Reprint, 1963. The reprint is taken from the copy used in the Public Record Office, which has many manuscript notes.

Norman sheriffs are listed in:

• GREEN, JUDITH A. *English sheriffs to 1154.* Public Record Office handbook **24**. HMSO, 1990.

A variety of county lists of sheriffs are available on the internet. See, for example:

• Sheriffs of the County of Kent
  www.british-history.ac.uk/report.aspx?compid=53762
• A List of the Mayors and Sheriffs of London from the earliest accounts
  www.british-history.ac.uk/report.aspx?compid=46797
• List of Sheriffs of the County of Cardigan (1540-1907)
  www.genuki.org.uk/big/wal/CGN/Sheriffs.html

D. Justices of the Peace

The names of Justices of the Peace can be found in a number of sources. They were appointed by commissions of the peace for an unspecified term. Fresh commissions were issued whenever the government wished to appoint a new member of the bench, or whenever it wished to remove one. Between 1625 and 1640, fifty-three of these commissions were issued for Somerset alone. They were probably sent to the Clerk of the Peace in each county, and can now be found amongst Quarter Sessions records, although they have not all survived.

Commissions of the Peace were issued under letters patent, and should have been enrolled on the patent rolls, now held in TNA, class C66. This was frequently done carelessly, sometimes not at all. Justices had to pay a fee for enrolment. This had to be kept at a low level, given that they were paying to be appointed to an office which might involve them in a lot of work for no remuneration, and that the frequency of new commissions made them rather ephemeral documents. Enrolment ceased in the 1670s.

The information on the patent roll was taken, not from the Commission itself, but from Crown Office entry books. These recorded all changes in the commission, including some not recorded in commissions, such as death or changes of status. They are similar to the *libri pacis*, which were compiled by the Crown Office for the use of the Treasury, the Privy Council, and other government agencies.

When a commission reached the Clerk of the Peace, he had to summon new members of the bench to appear at the next assizes to take their oaths, and to notify former JPs that their services were no longer required. He also had to draw up *nomina ministrorum* for the Assize judges. These were lists of the names of JPs, coroners, the escheators, bailiffs, high constables, and other officers who were expected to appear. These are the only lists of JPs which were compiled at regular intervals, and may be found either with Quarter Sessions records in county record offices, or with Assize records in the National Archives.

Justices of the Peace are also named in the *London gazette* **www.london-gazette.co.uk**, and in a wide range of other sources. Their attendance at each session are recorded in order books. They signed settlement examinations, removal orders, orders to overseers to bind pauper children as apprentices, and a range of other documents. Some of them kept their own justicing minute books. Occasionally, these and similar documents have been published. See, for example:

- CRITTALL, ELIZABETH, ed. T*he justicing notebook of William Hunt, 1744-1749.* Wiltshire Record Society, **37**. 1982.

Surviving lists of JPs, together with a detailed guide to the use of these lists, is provided in:

- BARNES, THOMAS G., & SMITH, A. HASSELL. 'Justices of the Peace from 1558 to 1688: a revised list of sources', *Bulletin of the Institute of Historical Research* **32**, 1959, pp.221-242.

The names of all Welsh JPs, together with a detailed guide to sources, are listed in:

- PHILLIPS, J. R. S. *The Justices of the Peace in Wales and Monmouthshire, 1541 to 1680.* University of Wales Press, 1975.

Further Reading

- GLEASON, J. H. *The Justices of the Peace in England, 1558 to 1640: a later eirenarcha.* Clarendon Press, 1969. This includes many lists of JPs for Kent, Northamptonshire, Somerset, Worcestershire, and the North Riding of Yorkshire in its appendices.
- LANDAU, NORMA. *The Justices of the Peace, 1679-1760.* University of California Press, 1984.
- GLASSEY, LIONEL K. J. *Politics and the appointment of Justices of the Peace, 1675-1720.* Oxford University Press, 1979.
- MOIR, ESTHER. *The Justice of the Peace.* Penguin, 1969.
- SKYRME, SIR THOMAS. *History of the Justices of the Peace.* 3rd ed. Chichester: Barry Rose, 1991.

E. The Lieutenancy and Militia

The defence of the realm was, for many centuries, dependent on the fact that every adult male was required to appear when called to serve in the militia. Henry VIII's use of this obligation to impose a tax in 1522 has already been considered. The requirements of the militia could be onerous. A 1558 statute required those with incomes of over £1000 to provide 16 horses, 80 suits of light armour 40 pikes, 30 longbows, 20 bills or balberds, 20 harquebuses, and 50 steel helmets[174]. Records of musters, such as those of 1569, bear witness to the burdens placed on the gentry.

Of equal significance, for our purposes, was the role of the gentry in commanding the militia. Supreme command was in the hands of the Lord Lieutenant, who was usually an aristocrat. His authority over the militia had been transferred from the sheriff during the reign of Edward VI. Lord Lieutenants became the principal representatives of the Crown in each county. They had a major influence in the appointment of JPs, and acquired considerable electoral influence. For a list of Lord Lieutenants, see:

- SAINTY, J. C. *Lieutenants of counties, 1585-1642.* Bulletin of the Institute of Historical Research special supplement **8**. 1970.
- SAINTY, J. C. *List of Lieutenants of Counties of England & Wales 1660-1974.* List & Index Society special series **12**. 1974.

In order to discharge their military responsibilities, Lord Lieutenants (or the Crown) appointed a number of deputy lieutenants from amongst the leading gentry. They were expected to conduct musters, maintain the efficiency of the militia, and charge their fellow gentry with arms and horse[175]. They served as colonels in the trained bands. Sir Edmund Brudenall, who died in 1585, was said to have spent more time on the affairs of the militia than on anything else[176]. Other captains were also drawn from the gentry, whether they had any experience of military affairs or not. They were chosen 'partly for their reputation in the county, partly for their knowledge in martiall sciences'[177]. The former was the most important; inexperience could be remedied by employing trained soldiers to offer advice, but it was thought better not to break the bond between gentlemen and tenant, between captain and militiamen.

Warrants for the appointment of deputy lieutenants, 1679-1782 can be found in TNA, class SP44. Appointments are also listed in the *London gazette* **www.london-gazette.co.uk** from 1665. A number of lieutenancy letter books have been published; See, for example:

- BOURGEOIS, E. J., ed. *A Cambridgeshire lieutenancy letterbook 1595 to 1605.* Cambridgeshire Records Society **12**. 1997.

Much information on the militia and the gentry's role in it can be found amongst the State Papers[178]. Genealogical information on Deputy Lieutenants is provided by:

- The Peerage.com: Index to Deputy Lieutenants
  www.thepeerage.com/index_deplt.htm

During the Civil War, struggle for control of the militia was the issue which first sparked armed dispute. Both sides appointed officers to raise forces. Charles I issued commissions of array appointing Arraymen who were to take charge of the raising of his forces in the counties. The names of those appointed in August 1641 were subsequently listed in a manuscript now amongst the Finch-Hatton manuscripts at

Northamptonshire Record Office[179]. Parliament's Militia Ordinance appointed its own Lords Lieutenants, together with Parliamentary Committee men who effectively governed the counties under its control[180]. Their names, together with the names of many others appointed to various offices by Parliamentary ordinances, are given in:

- FIRTH, C. H., & RAIT, R. S., eds. *Acts and ordinances of the Interregnum, 1642-1660*. 3 Vols. HMSO, 1911.

After the Restoration, in 1660, a standing army was established, and the importance of the Militia declined, so that it had virtually ceased to exist by the beginning of the eighteenth century. The absence of the army overseas during the Seven Years War (1742-1748), combined with the threat posed by Jacobites in the 1745 rebellion, led to the Militia Act 1757. This re-established the force, which was officered, as in previous centuries, by the gentry.

Militia officers are listed in various *Militia lists*, which began to be published regularly in the late eighteenth century. Records of their services are to be found in various War Office classes in TNA. Full details are given in:

- Armed forces: Militia 1757-1914
  www.nationalarchives.gov.uk/records/research-guides/armed-forces-1757-1914.htm

Officer's commissions were published in the *London gazette* **www.london-gazette.co.uk**. Lists of officers were also occasionally published as Parliamentary papers. See, for example:

- *Return of the names of the Colonels and other officers of the different regiments of militia in England and Wales, the dates of their commissions, listing those who have served in the Royal Household Brigade, the Line or the Royal Navy, 1839.* (HC1839 xxxi, 267).
- *Nominal return of officers holding commissions in Militia and in Volunteer Corps.* (HC1862; xxxii, 583).

For a detailed overview of militia records, see:

- SPENCER, WILLIAM. *Records of the militia & volunteer forces, 1757-1945: including records of the Volunteers, Rifle Volunteers, Yeomanry, Imperial Yeomanry, Fencibles, Territorials, and the Home Guard*. Rev ed. PRO Publications, 1997.

F. Escheators

Escheators were the officers responsible for ensuring that the Crown derived the maximum financial advantage from the feudal incidents that were its right. The word derived from the escheat, that is, property which reverted to its lord when a tenant died without heirs, or committed a felony, Escheators conducted *inquisitions post mortem* into the succession of tenants in chief[181], and *inquisitions ad quod damnum* to check how the king's interests would be affected by proposals to establish markets, alienate land to the church, or grant some other privilege. They could receive escheats of the lands of tenants in chief who had died, or pass information to the Court of Wards to ensure that the Crown's rights of wardship were respected. Escheators were usually gentlemen. The office ceased on the abolition of feudal tenure in 1660. Certificates of election of escheators can be found in TNA class C267 for 1303-1648, and C202 (1570-1660). They can also be identified directly from *inquisitions post mortem*. A list is provided by:

- WOOD, A. C. *List of escheators for England and Wales.* List & Index Society, **72**. 1971.

The other official who was required to be present at the taking of an *inquisition post mortem* was the feodary of the Court of Wards, who was tending to supplant the work of the escheator in the late sixteenth century[182]. His surveys of wards' estates provided the information which the Court needed before wardships were sold off. A number of sources for tracing feodaries are mentioned by Bell[183].

Bodley, William subscribed 11 July, 1623.

Bodley, Zachary, of ST. ALBAN HALL in or before 1572, clerk in holy orders, brother of Sir Thomas and Myles and Laurence.

Bodurda, Hugh, of co. Carnarvon, arm. HART HALL, matric. 30 May, 1589, aged 16.

Bodurda, John, of co. 'Carnarvon,' gent. HART HALL, matric. 7 April, 1609, aged 18.

Bodurda, William, of co. Carnarvon, gent. HART HALL, matric. 7 April, 1609, aged 16 ; B.A. 16 Nov., 1612, rector of Witton, in Droitwich, co. Worcester, 1622, and of South Wotton, Norfolk, 1624, until sequestered in 1646. See Foster's *Index Ecclesiasticus* & *Add. MS.*, 15,670, p. 71. **[5]**

Bodvell, John ; B.A. from ORIEL COLL. 17 Oct., 1594, M.A. 30 May, 1597, rector of (Llan) Edern, co. Carmarthen, 1597. See Foster's *Index Ecclesiasticus.*

Bodvell, John, of co. Carnarvon, arm. ORIEL COLL., matric. 14 Oct., 1597, aged 14 ; B.A. 29 April, 1602, (? created D.C.L. 20 Feb., 1643-4, see next entry), a student of the Inner Temple 1602, as of Bodville, co. Carnarvon, perhaps identical with the next named. See Foster's *Inns of Court Reg.*

Bodvill, John, created D.C.L. 20 Feb., 1643-4, M.P. co. Anglesey April to May 1640, and in long parliament 1640 till disabled 5 Feb., 1644, described in the parliamentary return as ' of Llanegrad,' sat also in the parliament at Oxford. See *Fasti*, ii. 66.

Body, John (Bodie) ; B.C.L. 1553, D.C.L. (sup. 24 Jan.) 1558-9 (? a student of the Inner Temple 1547). See Foster's *Inns of Court Reg.* & *Fasti*, i. 142, 199.

Body, John (Bodie) ; B.A. 11 July, 1554, M.A. 10 July, 1562, rector of Burnet, Somerset, 1564. See *Weaver.*

Body, John (Bodie), scholar of NEW COLL. 1567 ; B.A. (deid.) 1571-2, M.A. 1 Feb., 1575-6, removed from his fellowship 1577 for being a Papist, etc., ' at length executed at Andover 2 Nov., 1583, for denying the Queen's supremacy over the Church of England.' See *Fasti*, i. 199 ; *O.H.S.*, xii., 10. **[11]**

Bodycott, William, fellow of NEW COLL. 1497. from Andover, Hants ; B.C.L. 31 March, 1506, B.Can.L. 3 Feb., 1510-11, died in 1512.

85

Boehm, Sigismund, s. Clement, of London, gent. CHRIST CHURCH, matric. 9 July, 1709, aged 15 ; B.A. 1713, of Dunton Hall, co. Lincoln, sheriff 1723, a student of Middle Temple 1713, assumed the additional final surname of Trafford, died s.p. 1 Feb., 1740-1, buried at Tydd St. Mary. See Foster's *Lancashire Collections.*

Bogan. See also BOUGHEN.

Bogan, Walter, s. William, of Little Hempston, Devon, arm. CORPUS CHRISTI COLL., matric. 7 April, 1682, aged 18 ; of Gatcombe, buried at Little Hempston 24 Feb., 1702-3, brother of Zachary and father of William 1709. **[15]**

Bogan, William, s. William, of Little Hempston, Devon, gent. CORPUS CHRISTI COLL., matric. 24 March, 1636-7, aged 17 ; of Gatcombe, buried at Little Hempston, 3 June, 1681, brother of Zachary 1640, and father of Zachary 1682, and of Walter.

Bogan, William, s. Walter, of Gatcombe, Devon, arm. EXETER COLL., matric. 2 July, 1709, aged 17 ; buried at Little Hempston 10 Nov., 1725. See Vivian's *Visitation of Devon.*

Bogan, Zachary, s. William, of Hempston, Devon, gent. ST. ALBAN HALL, matric. 13 Nov., 1640, aged 13 ; scholar CORPUS CHRISTI COLL. 1641, B.A. 21 Oct., 1646, fellow 1647, M.A. 19 Nov., 1650, died 1 Sept., 1659, aged 34, brother of William 1637. See *Ath.*, iii. 476 ; *Gutch*, i. 413 ; *Burrows* & *D.N.B.*

Bogan, Zachary, s. William, of Little Hempston, Devon, arm. EXETER COLL., matric. 7 April, 1682, aged 16 ; B.A. 1685, buried at Little Hempston 2 Nov., 1693.

Boger, Michael ; B.A. (sup. 24 April) 1597. **[20]**

Boham, Hugh, s. Hugh, of Money-Ash, co. Derby, pleb. LINCOLN COLL., matric. 24 Oct., 1628, aged 15 (called Bohann in *Mat. Reg.*) ; B.A. 5 July, 1632 ; M.A. from ALL SOUL'S COLL. 20 June, 1636, created B.D. (1 or 2) Nov., 1642 (and query D.D. 16 Jan., 1642-3 as Bowen), expelled by the parliamentary visitors in 1648, rector of Harding *alias* Harpsden, Oxon, 1662, and of Whitwell, co. Derby, 1662. See Foster's *Index Ecclesiasticus* & *Burrows.*

Bohemia, Frederick, King of, Elector Palatine of the Rhine, Duke of Bavaria, subscribed in 1613, ' R. M. H. N. D. W. Fredericus Elector Palatinus,' married at Whitehall on St. Valentine's Day, 14 Feb., 1613, Elizabeth, eldest daughter of James I., died at Mentz 29 Nov., 1632. See *Fasti*, i. 351 ; *O.H.S.*, xi. 333 ; & Foster's *Peerage.*

Boherel, Elias, 1687. See *Fasti*, ii. 402.

Bohun, Ralph, pleb. NEW COLL., matric. 8 Dec., 1658, fellow 1658, B.C.L. 1665, D.C.L. 1685, rector of West Kington, Wilts, 1674, and of Wotton, Surrey, 1701, canon of Sarum 1701, died 12 July, 1716. See *Manning and Bray*, ii. 158n ; *Ath.*, iv. 549 ; *Fasti*, ii. 397 ; & Foster's *Index Ecclesiasticus.*

Bois. See BOYS. **[25]**

Bolday, John, of CORPUS CHRISTI COLL., 18 June, 1520, from Somerset ; B.A. 30 May, 1524, fellow 1524, M.A. 14 July, 1528. See *O.H.S.*, i. 307.

Bolde, Alexander ; B.D. Canterbury, incorp. 14 July, 1618.

Bold, Arthur, of co. Southampton, gent. MAGDALEN HALL, matric. 26 June, 1621, aged 17 ; bar.-at-law, Inner Temple, 1634, bencher 1658, Autumn Reader, 1663 (as son of Arthur, of Petersfield, co. Southants, gent.), M.P. Petersfield 1660, until his death in 1677. See Foster's *Judges and Barristers.*

Bold, Arthur, gent. MAGDALEN COLL., matric. 1 April, 1656, chorister 1651-5, a student of the Inner Temple 1657, as of Petersfield, aforesaid. See Foster's *Inns of Court Reg.* & *Bloxam*, i. 70.

Bolde, Edward (Bould), of co. Southampton, gent. MAGDALEN COLL., matric. 16 June, 1610, aged 17 ; demy 1608-18. B.A. 11 Feb., 1612-13, M.A. 3 July, 1616. See *Bloxam*, v. 31. **[30]**

Bold, Edward ; B.A. from BRASENOSE COLL., 7 July, 1624, M.A. 5 July, 1627, rector of Thurstaston, Cheshire, 1636-41, rector of Hawarden, Flints, 1641, buried in the parish church 5 Jan., 1655. See Foster's *Index Ecclesiasticus* & *Add. MS.*, 15,670.

Bolde, Henry (Bould), of co. Carnarvon, 'cler. fil.' JESUS COLL., matric. 1 June, 1621, aged 19 ; B.A. 19 Nov.. 1621, M.A. 1 July, 1624.

Bold, Henry, of co. Southampton, gent. MAGDALEN HALL, matric. 26 June, 1621, aged 19 ; B.A. from ST. MARY HALL 29 Oct., 1622, M.A. 22 June, 1625, incorp. at Cambridge 1628.

Bolde, Henry, s. William, of Petersfield, Hants, pleb. MAGDALEN COLL., matric. 7 March, 1622-3, aged 16 ; demy 1620-36, B.A. 7 Dec., 1626, M.A. 20 June, 1629, vicar of Willoughby, co. Warwick, 1636, deprived 1654, restored 1660, and resigned 1684, one of these names rector of Inkpen, Berks, 1651. See *Bloxam*, v. 106.

Bolde, Henry, 4s. William, of Newstead, Hants, fellow NEW COLL., from Winchester School 1645, ejected by the parliamentary visitors 1648, went 'to the great city,' entered the examiners office in Chancery, died 23 Oct., 1683, aged 56, buried in Twyford Church, Middlesex. See *Burrows* & *Ath.*, iv. 115.

Bold, Henry, gent. CHRIST CHURCH, matric. 7 July, 1651, student 1651, B.A. 24 Feb., 1654-5, M.A. 11 June, 1657, proctor 1662 (incorp. at Cambridge 1658), B.D. 5 July, 1664, chaplain to Lord Arlington, chaunter or precentor of Exeter with a prebend 1668, fellow of Eton 1669, died 9 Sept., 1677. See *Fasti*, ii. 278 ; *Alumni West.*, 126 ; & *D.N.B.* **[36]**

Bolde, John (Boolde), chaplain, B.Can.L, 3 July, 1528.

14. Alumini Oxonienses - The members of the University of Oxford 1500-1741:
Their peerage, birthplace and year of birth with a record of their degree ... by Joseph Foster 1891.

110

CHAPTER ELEVEN

Gentry Education and Gentlemanly Occupations

A. Education: Public Schools

Until the nineteenth century, education beyond the elementary stage was largely the preserve of the gentry. Public schools - those which attracted support from wide areas - were filled with gentlemen's sons. The great majority of University entrants in the sixteenth and seventeenth centuries had some formal education behind them[184]. Many public school founders had intended them to be open to all, but by the nineteenth century they were frequently expensive, and only for those who could afford to pay. They were regarded as a gentry preserve. However, as the industrial revolution progressed, the range of parents who could afford to pay widened. Public schools gradually opened their doors to sons of the new industrialists and self-made men. The aim of the reformed public schools of the Victorian era was 'to inculcate the sons of the newly enriched middle-class professional man, merchant, or banker, with the same moral values, religious beliefs, sense of duty, good breeding, and classical education as the sons of the gentry'[185]. That ultimately led the gentry to regard them as equals, at the same time as the relationship between wealth and land diminished in the late nineteenth and early twentieth centuries.

Pupils at public school were recorded in their registers. Many of these have been published; a comprehensive listing is provided by:

- JACOBS, P. M. *Registers of the universities, colleges and schools of Great Britain and Ireland.* Athlone Press, 1964.

An extensive collection of school registers is held by the Society of Genealogists. These are listed in:

- *School, university, and college registers and histories in the library of the Society of Genealogists.* 2nd ed. Society of Genealogists, 2006.

A number of published school registers can be searched at **www.ancestry.co.uk**.

B. Education: Universities

The universities were also the domain of the gentry. That did not necessarily mean that they took degrees or other qualifications. The eldest sons of the landed elite usually attended one of the universities, but rarely took degrees, and so did not matriculate. Their presence will therefore not be recorded in the various listings of alumni, although their younger brothers will be there[186]. Nevertheless, in the early seventeenth century, virtually all Gloucestershire JPs and MPs had studied at Oxford. There were usually about 25 sons of Glamorganshire gentry present in Oxford, from a county which only had 60 or 70 families with incomes of over £150 per annum[187]. Some families sent all their young men to particular colleges; indeed, some colleges were dominated by students from particular regions. The Cornish, for example, frequently attended Exeter College, Oxford.

15. A nineteenth-century gentleman's room at Trinity College, Oxford University (Wikimedia).

There are a number of biographical dictionaries of University alumni. These are based on matriculation records, which were not always well-kept, especially in earlier centuries[188]. They do, however, record many thousand students, and should be consulted by everyone interested in tracing gentle ancestors. See:

- EMDEN, A. B. *A biographical register of the University of Oxford to A.D. 1500.* 3 vols. Clarendon Press, 1957-1959. For corrections and additions, see *Bodleian Library record* **6**, 1957-1961, pp.668-688; **7**, 1962-1967, pp.149-164.
- EMDEN, A. B. *A biographical register of the University of Oxford, A.D. 1501-to 1540.* Clarendon Press, 1974. For corrections, see Margaret Bowker's review in *Archives,* **12**(53), 1975, pp.15-24.
- FOSTER, I. *Alumni Oxonienses 1500-1886.* 8 vols. Parker & Co., 1887-1892. Reprinted in 4 vols., Kraus Reprint, 1980. Also available at **www.ancestry.co.uk**
- FOSTER, JOSEPH. *Oxford Men 1880-1892, with a record of their Schools Honors and Degrees.* James Parker & Co., 1893. Also available at **www.ancestry.co.uk.**
- EMDEN, A. B. *A biographical register of the University of Cambridge to 1500.* Cambridge University Press, 1963.
- VENN, J., & VENN, J. A. *Alumni Cantabrigienses.* Pt. 1. [150]-1751 (4 vols). Pt 2. 1751-1900 (6 vols). Cambridge University Press, 1922-1954. Also available at **www.ancestry.co.uk**

There are also many registers devoted to particular colleges. These are worth seeking out, but are too many to list here. Some can be searched at **www.ancestry.co.uk**.

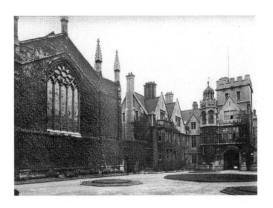

16. Brasenose College, Oxford (Wikimedia).

After the Reformation, the universities were only open to those who conformed to the doctrines of the Church of England. Roman Catholics and protestant dissenters were excluded. We need not concern ourselves here with dissenters, since the great majority were not gentry. However, Roman Catholicism in England depended on gentry support. Many gentlemen sent their young men to study at Catholic colleges abroad, despite the fact that to do so was illegal. These colleges had been founded as crusading institutions, in order to disseminate the doctrines of the Counter-Reformation in England. The earliest priests from Douai began to arrive in England in 1574; by 1580 over 100 had been sent. There were also English seminaries at Rome, Valladolid, Seville, Madrid, and Lisbon. Most of their Yorkshire students were younger sons of the gentry. It was rare for heirs to study overseas, in view of the risks[189].

A number of registers of seminary alumni, and other related documents, have been published by the Catholic Record Society **www.catholic-history.org.uk/crs**. See, for example[190]:

- SHARRATT, MICHAEL, ed. *Lisbon College Register, 1628-1813*. Catholic Record Society **72**. 1991.
- HOLT, G. *St Omers and Bruges Colleges, 1593-1773: A biographical dictionary*. Catholic Record Society **69**. 1979.

C. The Grand Tour and Overseas Travel

Roman Catholics were not the only people who travelled on the continent. They were followed by Royalist exiles between 1646 and 1660, and by former Parliamentarians after 1660. There were, however, more positive reasons for overseas travel than escaping the consequences of recusancy or 'delinquency'. In the late Tudor and Stuart periods, it gradually became fashionable for the heirs of wealthy gentry to travel on the Continent in order to complete their education. Lord Burleigh's advice to his son reflected his conservatism. 'Suffer not thy sons to pass the Alps, for they shall learn nothing but pride, blasphemy, and atheism. And if by travel they attain to some few broken languages, they will profit them no more than to have one meat served in divers dishes'. His advice was increasingly not followed[191]. Between 1558 and 1642, over 100 Yorkshire heirs travelled on the Continent in order to acquire languages, art, antiquities, and 'polish'[192]. Others went to visit relatives, to conduct business, or to take the waters at Spa. Numbers increased in subsequent centuries. Many associated themselves with English diplomats overseas, accompanying them on their travels - and thus both adding prestige to embassies, and securing a safer journey. Others went as volunteers to fight in the Low Countries, before using their military training to return home and fight in the English civil war. Gentlemen's travels are frequently recorded in Privy Council registers. These record the grant of passes which state the purpose of overseas travel. The registers are printed for the period 1542-1631 as:

- DASENT, JOHN ROCHE, ed. *Acts of the Privy Council of England.* 46 vols. H.M.S.O., 1890-1964.

Records of licences to 'pass beyond the seas' - early forms of passports - can also be found in a variety of other TNA classes. A brief guide to these is included in:

- Passport Records
  www.nationalarchives.gov.uk/records/research-guides/passports.htm

For a detailed discussion of the Grand Tour, together with many notes on sources (including manuscript diaries), see:

- STOYE, JOHN. *English travellers abroad 1604-1667.* Rev. ed. Yale University Press, 1989.

A biographical dictionary of (mainly) gentle travellers in Italy is provided by:

- INGAMELLS, JOHN. *A dictionary of British and Irish travellers in Italy, 1701-1800.* Yale University Press for the Paul Mellon Centre, 1997.

Those who went to Padua to study are listed in:

- BROWN, HORATIO F. *Inglesi e Scozzesi all'Università di Padova dall'anno 1618 sino al 1765.* Venezia, 1921.

D. Gentlemanly Careers

Most gentlemen were fully occupied with running their estates, serving as unpaid administrators, and riding to hounds. Some, however, did not have sufficient income to live as a gentleman should. Edward Chamberlayne, writing in 1669, observed that, amongst the gentry, 'younger brothers ... have small estates in land, but are commonly bred up to divinity, law, physick, to Court and military employment, but of late too many of them to shop-keeping'[193]. Sir John Oglander went as far as to argue that 'it is impossible for a mere country gentleman ever to grow rich or raise his house. He must have some other vocation with his inheritance, as to be a courtier, lawyer, merchant or some other vocation'[194]. His words applied more to the smaller landed gentry than to those with wide estates. Nevertheless, a quarter of the heads of Yorkshire gentry families had professional or commercial occupations[195]. In London, the visitation pedigrees of 1687 (many of which related to tradesmen) repeatedly trace the claims of Londoners to gentility back through the generations to provincial England [196].

The comments of Chamberlayne and Oglander ignored the fact that the landed elite frequently acquired their wealth originally from sources other than land[197]. Relatively few new entrants to the landed elite based their wealth solely on land[198]. In the sixteenth and seventeenth centuries, many office holders entered the elite. In the eighteenth century, judges and other lawyers were in an excellent position to acquire the necessary wealth. During the wars of the eighteenth and nineteenth centuries, senior military and naval personnel amassed enough wealth to purchase large estates. So did East India Company nabobs and other overseas merchants. In the nineteenth century, they were joined by many bankers, scriveners, and business men from the City of London. Brewers could also make a lot of money, but few other manufacturers joined the elite until the late nineteenth century.

Many gentlemen were forced to recognise the economic reality that they had to earn their own livings. Their younger sons in particular frequently needed to do so. Their position has been described as 'inherently uncomfortable and unstable'[199]. The sour comment of Thomas Wilson encapsulates their predicament: 'He [the eldest son] must have all, and all the rest that which the cat left on the malt heape'[200]. A side effect of the system of primogeniture and the strict settlement was the creation of a class of well-educated gentlemen, used to the country house, who lacked the means to live in the style to which they were accustomed. This class gradually colonised the army, the church, and the law, and played an important role in the growth of the professions in the nineteenth century. They created the idea of professionalism.

There were a number of major career routes open to gentlemen's sons. The life of a courtier had the greatest prestige, and sometimes the greatest rewards - but it was very risky. The army, the church, the law, and medicine, were all accepted as gentlemanly occupations. There was a tendency to destine the second son for the law, the third, for the church, and the last for trade. Trade was the least acceptable profession for a gentleman, but nevertheless apprenticeships became increasingly popular amongst the gentry in the eighteenth and nineteenth centuries. Even at the end of the seventeenth century, between 16% and 30% of apprentices entering the more prestigious merchant guilds of London were the sons of gentlemen; 10% of those admitted to the freedom of the City in 1690 were the sons of knights or gentlemen[201]. Admittedly, many of these were from the minor gentry, rather than from the possessors of large estates. The Barnardiston family of Suffolk were an exception to this rule; no less than 5 sons of the great puritan squire, Sir Nathaniel Barnardiston, went into commerce. He 'was ever importunate to have all his sons employed, not taking it as becoming to have any of his line out of useful callings'[202]. For other wealthy gentry, the only apprenticeship which agreed with their status was with one of the great trading companies, such as the East India Company, or the Levant

Company. Such apprenticeships might cost £1000+, on top of which a further £1000 might be needed for working capital when the apprenticeship was at an end[203].

These trading companies also attracted direct investment from the gentry. It was not necessary to serve an apprenticeship in order to make money from them. For example, Sir John Hotham of Scorborough had money invested in the East India Company when he died in 1645[204]. There were usually some 2,000 proprietors; only those with £1000 or more invested were entitled to take part in ballots[205]. In 1795, there were 25 of these in Hampshire alone[206].

In the following sections, sources for the major professions open to gentlemen are briefly outlined. For most of these professions, much more detailed handbooks and guides for the family historian are available, and these are noted as appropriate. Since this book is devoted to gentlemen, I have restricted my coverage of the late nineteenth and twentieth centuries. In this period the middle classes were taking over the professions.

E. Courtiers and Office Holding

Many gentry attended the King's court for shorter or longer periods. Life as a courtier was both expensive and risky - but sometimes it led to great rewards. The Crown had many offices and lands in its gift. Office usually meant the opportunity to levy fees, and to seek gratuities from those who needed your favour. It might also give the holder the ability to indulge in what is now known as insider trading. Many of those close to the Court of Augmentations (which was responsible for administering properties seized by Henry VIII) in the mid-sixteenth century benefited from the information that their position provided, and made their fortune from purchasing monastic property.

If you could attract the interest of a King or Queen, your fortune could be made. Sometimes, recognition was deserved: John Russell[207] was an obscure Dorset gentleman until, in 1506, a storm at sea forced the King and Queen of Castille to land at Melcombe Regis. Russell escorted them to the court of Henry VII as an interpreter, came to Henry's notice, and was appointed by him as a gentleman of the Chamber. He rose rapidly in the royal service, eventually being made Earl of Bedford, and given wide acres of monastic property to support his dignity. He was an efficient administrator and soldier, and bore responsibility for defeating the Prayer Book Rebellion in 1549.

Less deserving was George Villiers, the younger son by a second marriage of a minor Leicestershire gentleman[208]. When he began his courtly career, his sole asset was an annuity of £50. Villiers became the rather dubious favourite of James I, who made him Duke of Buckingham and Lord High Admiral. In the end, however, he suffered for his success: he was assassinated.

More modest success was achieved by Sir Thomas Cornwallis[209] of Brome, one of the Suffolk gentlemen who supported Mary Tudor's rebellion in 1553. He was rewarded with a seat on Mary's Council, together with a number of grants of lands and wardships. When the Queen died in 1558, he retired to his estates, having made some useful additions to his income. His subsequent recusancy did not seriously damage his finances.

Many other gentry held government office. Most of Charles I's administrators held armigerous rank; 68% were landowners. It has been estimated that one in every eight or ten knights, and one in every sixteen esquires, held some office[210]. The Crown had in its gift all major offices, many of middle rank, and a few minor posts. Occasionally, it was the sovereign himself who made the choice; more frequently, he gave formal approval to a choice already made by the head of the department concerned, or by some other minister. He also paid heed to the importunities of suitors and court favourites. Many middle ranking and junior positions in government service were appointed by the head of their office. There were frequent disputes about who had the right to appoint to a particular position. For example, Sir Julius Caesar, master of the rolls, sought to appoint one of his sons to a vacant Six Clerkship in the Court of Chancery. The Lord Treasurer, however, persuaded the king to make him accept a different candidate - who paid £6000 for the Clerkship.

Appointment did not depend on merit, although that may have influenced career progression. Those seeking appointment depended on knowing someone who could press their case in the right quarters. Sir Allen Apsley secured his position in Queen Elizabeth's Household 'by means of a relation at court', according to his daughter[211]. It would have been extremely difficult for anyone to secure an appointment without knowing a courtier or office-holder. Those in power could exercise their rights of patronage to build up their own power base, and to ensure that their supporters filled government positions. Their ability to do so enabled them to charge for the privilege. Sir Henry Vane commenced his career as a royal Carver; he paid £5000 for the position[212]. Allegiance to a particular minister, and/or the ability to pay them, were the routes to a career in government service. When Leoline Jenkins and Francis Gwyn, both gentlemen of Glamorganshire, became secretaries of state, Squire Morgan of Coedygoras was able to write to them inquiring 'whether there be in the disposal of either of you any place that may be in any way advantageous to his eldest son'[213]. It was also possible to purchase an office from the existing holder, from the head of the relevant department, or from the holder of a reversion. The role of the

Duke of Buckingham as broker in chief of the trade in offices under James I is well-known[214].

Patronage and purchase were not the only means of securing an office. A few offices, such as that of Earl Marshall, and the Marshall of Common Pleas, were hereditary[215] (the Earl Marshall still is). Others, although not hereditary in theory, were so in practice. Office holders could easily secure a reversion of their office in favour of a son or other relative. In 1640, for example, the Surveyor Generalship of the Customs in the Outports was re-granted to three members of the Dawes family, on the surrender of an earlier grant to two of them[216]. Senior figures could easily find offices for their sons: Sir Thomas Jermyn, a Privy Councillor in the 1630s, secured reversions of the Clerkship of the Pipe, the Clerkship of writs and enrolments in King's Bench, the Attorneyship and Coronership of Kings Bench, the Keepership of books and orders in Chancery, the Surveyorship of the petty Customs of London, the Governorship of Jersey, and the Keepership of Hampton Court Park, for his young offspring[217].

For a detailed study of crown officials (which the foregoing paragraphs are based on), see:

- AYLMER, GEOFFREY. *The King's servants: the civil service of Charles I., 1625-1642*. Routledge & Kegan Paul, 1961. This is continued for the Interregnum in:
- AYLMER, G. E. *The state's servants: the civil service of the English Republic, 1649-1660* Routledge & Kegan Paul, 1973.

Local offices were also important to the gentry. The administration of crown estates, for example, those of the Duchy of Lancaster, required many officials - manors required bailiffs, stewards, and receivers; forests required bow bearers, master of game, and keepers of parks; castles required constables[218]. Such positions carried with them many perquisites, which were frequently more valuable than the actual fees. For example, the steward of the manor of Wakefield was usually granted a lease of the mills and bailiwick of Wakefield, worth £450 per annum[219]. Frequently, the work involved was delegated to servants. For office holders in the Duchy, see:

- SOMERVILLE, ROBERT. *History of the Duchy of Lancaster, volume 1. 1265-1603*. Chancellor & Council of the Duchy of Lancaster, 1953.
- SOMERVILLE, ROBERT. *Office-holders in the Duchy and County Palatine of Lancaster from 1603*. Phillimore, 1972.

A wide variety of grants from the Crown can be found on the Patent Rolls (class C66) in TNA. These run from 1201 to 1946, and are fully described by:

- Royal grants: letters patent and charters from 1199
  www.nationalarchives.gov.uk/records/research-guides/royal-grants.htm

The rolls prior to 1452 can be searched at:

- Calendar of Patent Rolls
  http://sdrc.lib.uiowa.edu/patentrolls/search.html.
  This database is based on published volumes. The subsequent period to 1608 is also covered in these volumes, the most recent of which have been published by the List & Index Society.

See also:

- *Exchequer, Augmentation Office letters patent (original) E313/1-14): index of persons and subjects: Henry III-Charles I.* List & Index Society, **185**. 1982.
- WILKINSON, LOUISE. 'Completing the calendar of Patent Rolls, Elizabeth I', *Local historian* 35(1), 2005, pp.30-43.

It may also be worth consulting the fine rolls (class C60 in TNA). These include many documents issued under the Great Seal relating to matters in which the Crown had a direct financial interest, such as grants of office, and licences to alienate lands held in chief of the Crown. The rolls take their name from the enrolment on them of fines, i.e. payments made to the Crown for licences, grants, writs, etc. Medieval fine rolls covering the period 1272-1609 have been calendared:

- *Calendar of the fine rolls preserved in the Public Record Office.* 22 vols. HMSO, 1911-1962.

The fine rolls for the reign of Henry III have been digitised:

- Henry III Fine Rolls Project
  www.finerollshenry3.org.uk

The state papers domestic are the archives of the Secretaries of State. These documents cover the period from 1547 to 1782, and deal with an extraordinarily wide range of topics, including much biographical information. See:

- State Papers Domestic: Edward VI-Charles I 1547-1649
  www.nationalarchives.gov.uk/records/research-guides/state-papers-1547-1649.htm
  A number of further pages cover subsequent periods up to 1782.

A microfilm edition of these papers is widely available in libraries:

- *The complete state papers domestic.* Many microfilm reels plus a booklet. Harvester Press, 1977.

These papers are also available online (unfortunately to institutions only) at:

- State Papers Online
  http://gale.cengage.co.uk/state-papers-online-15091714.aspx

Published calendars are widely available:

- *Calendar of state papers, domestic series of the reigns of Edward VI, Mary, Elizabeth [and James I], 1547-1625.* 12 vols. HMSO, 1866-1877. Many further volumes continue the series up to 1704. Some of these are available online at: **www.british-history.ac.uk/catalogue.aspx?type=3**

For an earlier series of similar papers, see:

- *Calendar of letters and papers, foreign and domestic, Henry VIII. 21 vols. 1864-1932.* These are also available online at: **www.british-history.ac.uk/ catalogue.aspx?type=3**

Another potentially valuable source of information on courtiers are the lists of royal office holders compiled by Sir John Sainty. These cover a very wide range of offices, including, for example, the Exchequer, the Mint, and the Royal Household. Each of these establishments had a wide range of staff; for example, the officers in the household of Princess Augusta between 1736-1772 included her Vice Chamberlain/ Chamberlain, the Groom of the Stole and Mistress of Robes, her maids and pages of honour, the Ladies and Women of her Bedchamber, her laundress, the Gentlemen Ushers of Privy Chamber, her Gentleman Ushers, Daily Waiters, and Quarterly Waiters, her Treasurer, the Clerks of her Household, her Secretary, Auditor, Clerk of the Closet, Physicians, Surgeons, and Apothecary, the Commissioner of her Stables, and her Equerries. Sainty's lists have been published, and are now available on-line:

- Office-Holders in Modern Britain
  www.history.ac.uk/publications/office

For officers of the royal household, see:

- Database of Court Officers 1660-1837
  www.luc.edu/history/fac_resources/bucholz/DCO/DCO.html

Office holders are also listed in:

- HAYDN, JOSEPH. *Haydn's book of dignities.* Bath: Firecrest Publishing, 1969. Originally published as 3rd ed., W. H. Allen, 1894.

F. The Army

Until the First World War, officers of the British Army were usually gentlemen. A detailed discussion of sources for army officers would be superfluous here. There are many books that provide the information needed by researchers. Some of the most useful include:

- WATTS, MICHAEL J., & WATTS, CHRISTOPHER T. *My ancestor was in the British Army: how can I find out more about him?* 2nd ed. Society of Genealogists Enterprises, 2009.
- SPENCER, WILLIAM. *Family history in the wars: how your ancestors served their country.* National Archives, 2007.
- FOWLER, SIMON. *Tracing your army ancestors.* Pen & Sword, 2006.

For the First World War, Norman Holding has written three complementary guides:

- HOLDING, NORMAN. *World War I army ancestry.* 4th ed. Rev. by Iain Swinnerton. Federation of Family History Societies, 2003.
- HOLDING, NORMAN. *More sources of World War I army ancestry.* 3rd ed. Federation of Family History Societies, 1998.
- HOLDING, NORMAN. *The location of British Army records.* 4th ed., rev. by Iain Swinnerton. Federation of Family History Societies, 1999.

See also:

- FOWLER, SIMON. *Tracing your First World War ancestors.* New ed. Countryside Books, 2008.
- SPENCER, WILLIAM. *Army service records of the First World War.* Public Record Office, 2001.

There are numerous lists of officers, and much other pertinent information, in the numerous regimental histories which have been published. These are listed in:

• WHITE, ARTHUR S. *A bibliography of regimental histories of the British Army.* Society for Army Historical Research, 1965.

Some general remarks are worth making. For our present purposes, the records of army officers can be divided into two groups: the Civil War, and the period from the early eighteenth century until the First World War. In the first period, there was no standing army until Cromwell's New Model Army was established. Regiments were raised by leading gentry from amongst their own tenants and retainers. Sir Edward Stradling, who raised one of the regiments that fought at Edgehill, and Sir Bevill Grenville, who died at the Battle of Lansdowne, were both commissioned by the Crown, raised their own regiments, and appointed their own officers - most of whom were minor gentry. Some Parliamentary officers are listed in muster rolls and pay lists held by TNA (in E315 and SP28/120-25). Many officers of both sides are listed in:

• PEACOCK, EDWARD. *The army lists of the Roundheads and Cavaliers: containing the names of the officers in the royal and parliamentary armies of 1642.* 2nd ed. Chatto & Windus, 1874. Reprinted Ken Trotman, 1983.

See also:

• REID, STUART. *Officers and regiments of the Royalist Army: being a revised edition of the List of indigent officers, 1663.* Leigh-on-Sea: Partizan Press, [1988].
• NEWMAN, P. R. 'The 1663 list of indigent Royalist officers considered as a primary source for the study of the Royalist army', *Historical journal* **30**, 1987, pp.887-889.

A variety of sources for Civil War officers are discussed in:

• Civil War Soldiers 1642-1660
  www.nationalarchives.gov.uk/catalogue/researchguidesindex.asp

Warrants for officers' commissions after 1660 are likely to be in the *Calendar of state papers domestic*[220]. Manuscript lists of officers between 1702 and 1752 can be found in TNA, class WO 64. An officer's career after 1754 is most easily traced through the published *Army lists*. There are a variety of other sources which can be used to trace officers and their families. TNA has many useful 'in depth research guides' on its website at **www.nationalarchives.gov.uk/records/research-guides.** Amongst others, these include:

- British Army: officers' records 1660-1913
- British Army Lists
- British Army: auxiliary forces 1769-1945
- British Army: campaign records 1660-1714
- British Army: campaign records 1714-1815
- British Army: campaign records 1816-1913
- British Army: First World War officers' records
- British Army: muster rolls and pay lists c.1730-1898
- British Army: officers' commissions
- British Army: officers' records 1660-1913
- British Army: soldiers' discharge and pension records 1702-1913
- British Army: tracing soldiers

The First World War was at least partially responsible for the end of gentry rule. It resulted in enormous number of casualties. The term 'the lost generation' is frequently used to describe its effect. The term is hyperbole, but it is understandable hyperbole. The men who formed the officer corps during the war were mostly gentlemen's sons, the men who aspired to set the tone of British culture and society in the 1920s and 1930s. In the first year of the war alone, 14% of officers died, compared to 6% of the rank and file[221]. The higher your social rank, the more likely you were to die in the war.

The first place to look for World War I gentry casualties is:

- *Officers who died in the Great War, 1914-1919.* Naval & Military Press, 2003. This is also available as an online pay-per-view database from **www.military-genealogy.com , www.ancestry.co.uk,** and **www.findmypast.co.uk**

There are innumerable published lists of men who served in the Army. These cannot all be listed here. University men, and members of the Inns of Court, were predominantly from the gentry. Their names are listed in:

- CAREY, G. V., ed. *The war list of the University of Cambridge.* Cambridge, 1920.
- CRAIG, E. S., & GIBSON, W. M., eds. *Oxford University roll of service.* Oxford, 1920.
- DARLING, C. *Inner Templars who volunteered and served in the Great War.* 1924.
- *The war book of Gray's Inn.* 1921.

G. The Church

Until the Reformation, a career in the church did not require much education. One of the major complaints of the reformers was that parish priests were frequently unlearned, and had not been trained for their position. Most came from humble backgrounds. The few who had degrees frequently had several rich livings, and spent their careers in ecclesiastical and/or royal administration.

After the Reformation, clergy were increasingly expected to be graduates. The emphasis that was placed on preaching by the reformers meant that priests were required to preach, and consequently needed adequate training. The need for learned priests was a serious problem for the early reformers; however, the increasing demand for graduate clergy meant that, by the eighteenth century, a career as a clergyman increasingly appealed to the younger sons of the gentry. A commentator writing in 1607 argued that the nobility and gentry would rather their sons became anything so long as they did not take holy orders. The prejudice did not long survive the fact that, at the Reformation, the nobility and gentry had acquired most of the advowsons formerly owned by monastic houses. Monasteries had owned many of the choicest livings in the church. Ownership allowed the gentry to solve the problem of how to provide for their younger sons and other relatives, without great expense. A good church living, formerly used to support a monastic establishment, would permit the incumbent to live as a gentleman should. Even in the seventeenth century, a clergyman such as John Porter at Ashton (Derbyshire) could make 'some pretence to magnificence': he had a set of leather chairs in his parlour, and no less than nine maps and seventeen framed pictures on his walls[222]. By 1790, a list of 109 major Glamorganshire landowners included ten clergymen[223].

A fairly typical example of the relationship between a gentle family and the clergy is provided by the Grenville family of Stowe, who owned much property in North Cornwall and North West Devon. Amongst their possessions was the advowson of their own parish of Kilkhampton. This enabled them to present four members of their own family for institution as rectors between 1294 and 1726. One, John Grenville, instituted in 1524, also held the local livings of Launcells (from 1536), Morwenstow (from 1541) and Week St Mary (from 1558). Another, Dennis Grenville (youngest son of Sir Bevill Grenville), became Dean of Durham in 1686 before going into exile with James II in 1688[224].

The number of clergy from gentry families increased in the eighteenth and nineteenth centuries, as the younger sons of the elite took advantage of the stranglehold which their parents had on ecclesiastical patronage[225]. No less than 17 members of the Gamage family became clergy between 1621 and 1740, making use of the advowsons in their families' possession, and following each other in some of Glamorganshire's richest livings[226]. The social standing of the clergy steadily increased. The first parish priest in Somerset to be made a JP was appointed in 1623. The absenteeism of local gentry encouraged the appointment of clerical JPs in late eighteenth century

Glamorganshire. By the nineteenth century, the clerics were amongst the most active members of the bench[227].

There are many sources where clergymen can be traced. These sources can sometimes also be used to trace the patrons of livings, the owners of advowsons. Here, it is only possible to provide a brief summary of sources for tracing the clergy.

An aspiring clergyman had first to be ordained by a bishop as a deacon, and then, a few years later as a priest. Many served a curacy for a few years before seeking their own benefice. They then had to find a patron owning the advowson of a living, who could present them to the bishop for institution. Ordinations, curacies, presentations, and institutions should all be recorded in registers and papers held amongst diocesan archives (usually held in local record offices). Many antiquarians have compiled lists of incumbents, which are frequently displayed in churches; substantial collections of these lists may be found in local record offices and local studies libraries, and some have been published. However, for the period 1540 to 1835, they are currently being steadily superseded by a new online database:

- Clergy of the Church of England Database
  www.theclergydatabase.org.uk/reference/links.html

This database is being compiled from the diocesan archives just mentioned. It aims to identify and list the major events of clerical careers - ordinations, appointments as curates and lecturers, institutions as rectors and vicars. As yet, not all dioceses are covered. After 1858, clergymen can easily be traced in *Crockford's clerical directory,* which continues to be regularly published, and provides basic information on clerical careers.

Many gentlemen's sons became senior clergy - bishops, deans, archdeacons, etc. These are listed in a series of volumes originally compiled by John Le Neve in the eighteenth century. A second edition of this work was compiled in the nineteenth century, and the twentieth century has seen a much more comprehensive re-compilation. For details of this work, and for a partial database, visit:

- Fasti Ecclesiae Anglicana
  www.history.ac.uk/publications/fasti

Two works give details of several thousand clergy who were ejected from their livings during and after the civil war:

- WALKER, A. G., ed. *Walker revised, being a revision of John Walker's Sufferings of the clergy during the Great Rebellion, 1642-1660.* Clarendon Press, 1948.

- WALKER, A. G., ed. *Calamy revised, being a revision of Edmund Calamy's Account of the ministers and others ejected and silenced, 1660-1662.* Clarendon Press, 1934.

A comprehensive guide to clergy records is provided by another volume in the present series:

- TOWEY, PETER. *My ancestor was an Anglican clergyman.* Society of Genealogists Enterprises, 2006.

Reference may also be made to:

- Lambeth Palace Library Research Guide: Biographical Sources for Anglican Clergy **www.lambethpalacelibrary.org/files/Clergy_Guide.pdf**

- Sources for Tracing Clergy and Lay Persons **www.history.ac.uk/gh/clergy.htm**

For the historical background, consult:

- O'DAY, ROSEMARY. *The English clergy: the emergence and consolidation of a profession, 1558-1642.* Leicester University Press, 1979.
- O'DAY, ROSEMARY, & HEAL, FELICITY. *Princes and paupers in the English church 1500-1800.* Leicester University Press, 1981.

The Church of England was not the only denomination which attracted gentry recruits to its ministry. Many sons of the Roman Catholic gentry also entered the ministry - in their case, clandestinely. Missionary priests, Jesuits, monks, and nuns, were all recruited from gentry families. It has already been seen how many Catholics were educated abroad. They frequently went on to the priesthood. A number of detailed biographical dictionaries list them[228]:

- BELLENGER, AIDAN. *English & Welsh priests 1558-1800: a working list.* Downside Abbey, 1984.
- FITZGERALD-LOMBARD, CHARLES. *English and Welsh priests 1800-1914: a working list.* Downside Abbey, 1993.
- ANSTRUTHER, G. *The seminary priests: a dictionary of the secular, clergy of England and Wales, 1558-1850.* 4 vols. St Edmunds College / Mayhew-McCrimmon, 1969-77.

H. The Law

The law was a perfectly respectable career option for impecunious younger sons of the gentry. It has been described as 'a powerful social and economic escalator'[229]. Newly enriched lawyers such as Richard Brownlow, chief notary of the Common Pleas, annoyed more established families. The Earl of Lincoln described him as a 'villayne' because he 'purchased land every day from under his nose and ... would purchase Sempringham Hall if he were suffered'[230].

Training in the law was not just for lawyers. All gentlemen needed a basic smattering of legal knowledge in order to serve as Justices of the Peace, to administer their estates, and to defend themselves against litigation. The Inns of Court, where lawyers received their training, attracted many young men who were not intending to practise law,. Many gentlemen finished off their education by spending some time there. Families frequently established connections with particular Inns; thus several members of the Hungerford family of Gloucestershire attended Lincoln's Inn; young men of the Dutton family attended the Inner Temple[231].

Gentlemen who attended the Inns of Court are recorded in their admission registers, a number of which have been printed. See:

- FOSTER, JOSEPH. *The register of admissions to Gray's Inn, 1521-1889, together with the register of marriages in Gray's Inn Chapel 1695-1754.* Hansard Publishing Union, 1889.
- BAILDON, WILLIAM. *Records of the Honourable Society of Lincoln's Inn: admissions 1420-1893, and chapel registers.* 2 vols. Lincoln s Inn, 1896.
- STURGESS, H. A. C. *Register of admissions to the Honourable Society of the Middle Temple, from the fifteenth century to the year 1944.* Butterworth, for the Society, 1949.

Admissions to the Inner Temple, 1547-1850 are listed by:

- The Inner Temple Admissions Database
  www.innertemple.org.uk/archive/itad/index.asp

The Inns of Chancery were also important. According to Brooks & Herber, they were originally 'preparatory schools for students intending to enter one of the Inns of Court, although they later degenerated into little more than social clubs, before disappearing altogether'[232]. Not many records survive for most of these Inns; however, two admissions registers have been transcribed:

- CARR, CECIL, ed. *Pension book of Clement's Inn.* Selden Society, **78**. 1960. Covers 1714-50, with list of members admitted 1656-1883.
- BROOKS, CHRISTOPHER, ed. *The admissions registers of Barnard's Inn, 1620-1869.* Selden Society supplementary series, **12**. 1995.

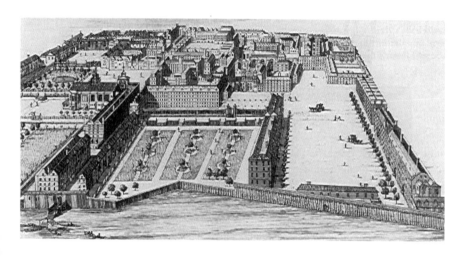

17. Two of the Inns of Court: The Inner Temple and the Outer Temple in 1720 (Wikimedia).

If the students at the Inns of Court wished to make their career in the law, there were many openings for them. The central courts steadily expanded their work, and required ever increasing numbers of trained officials such as judges and clerks. These offices could be very lucrative. The office of one of the Six Clerks in Chancery was worth about £1400 per year; under James I, the Clerks had to pay £6000 to be appointed[233]. Sir Rowland Wandesford, the eldest son of a Yorkshire gentleman, probably made about £1500 per annum as attorney of the Court of Wards[234]. The courts also needed barristers to plead before them, and bailiffs to ensure that their orders were enforced. In the localities, there was a need for scriveners to write deeds, for stewards to conduct manorial courts and the business of estates, for escheators to conduct *inquisitions post mortem*, for under sheriffs to conduct the business of the sheriff. When land was a measure of social standing, litigation was 'a constant past-time for those who lived on it'[235]. Efficiency was important if an estate was to prosper; the increased wealth of landed estates in Glamorganshire at the end of the eighteenth century has been attributed to the skill and diligence of the legally trained stewards who ran them, and who, in many cases, were able to acquire their own landed estates. The Edmondes family, stewards of the Aubreys of Llantrithyd (Glamorganshire), were able to purchase the Beaupre estate in 1755, and were said to be richer than their masters[236].

Lawyers, like the armed forces, have been the subject of many published listings. The earliest *Law list* was published in 1775. These lists began as simple lists of the names and addresses of lawyers. Further information was gradually added - years of admission, identification of the court(s) in which particular lawyer practised, official positions held, etc. They have been issued by various publishers at differing intervals over the last two centuries or so, and are easy to use to trace a particular individual's career. Law lists can be found in many reference libraries; particularly good collections are held by the Society of Genealogists, Guildhall Library, TNA, and the British Library. The Society of Genealogists holds a partial index to some early law lists; so does the Law Society.

Lawyers performed a wide range of different functions, and many specialised in a particular area, such as civil law (practised in the ecclesiastical courts). Legal training was needed by the stewards of manors, coroners, clerks of the peace, barristers, scriveners, and many other specialists. A number of biographical dictionaries and lists have been published for various different specialties. Judges are listed in:

- SAINTY, JOHN, SIR. *The judges of England, 1272-1990: a list of judges of the superior courts.* Selden Society supplementary series **10**. 1993.

For barristers who became King's Counsel (or Queen's Counsel), consult:

- SAINTY, JOHN. *A list of English law officers, King's Counsel, and holders of patents of precedence.* Supplementary series **7**. Selden Society, 1987.

Serjeants at law are identified in:

- BAKER, J. H. *The order of Serjeants at Law: a chronicle of creations, with related texts and a historical introduction.* Selden Society supplementary series 5. 1984.

Clerks of the Peace are listed in:

- STEPHEN, EDGAR. *The clerks of the counties 1360-1960.* Society of Clerks of the Peace of Counties and of Clerks of County Councils, 1961.

For scriveners, consult:

- STEER, FRANCIS W., ed. *Scriveners' Company common paper, 1357-1628, with a continuation to 1678.* London Record Society, **4**. 1968.

A wide range of other sources are available. Court records contain information about the lawyers who practised in them. The records of most central courts, and of Assizes, are held by TNA **www.nationalarchives.gov.uk**[237]. They also hold the records of the Prerogative Court of Canterbury, although the records of most other ecclesiastical courts are held in local record offices. Quarter Sessions records are also in local record offices, whilst the records of manorial courts are held in a variety of different repositories. For details, consult the Manorial Documents Register **www.nationalarchives.gov.uk/mdr**. The records of coroners can by found in both local record offices and TNA; see:

- GIBSON, JEREMY, & ROGERS, COLIN. *Coroners' records in England and Wales.* 3rd ed. Family History Partnership, 2010.

Law reports are another source which may be useful in identifying lawyers and the cases in which they were involved. These reports of cases where significant legal principles were involved have been regularly published for the use of lawyers since medieval times. As well as details of the cases themselves, they also identify the judges who heard the cases, and the barristers who acted. A variety of different series of law reports have been regularly published; these are listed in:

- *Guide to law reports and statutes.* 4th ed. Sweet & Maxwell, 1962.

Most law reports, unfortunately, do not index the lawyers involved. However, many early 'year books' have been published by the Selden Society **www.selden-society.qmw.ac.uk**, and are fully indexed.

The nineteenth century witnessed the commencement of a number of legal journals, which frequently mentioned individual lawyers. The *Law Journal* (1822-1965), the *Law Times* (1843-1965), and the *Solicitor's journal* (1857-) all carried information about lawyers which would be useful to family historians. Obituaries in the *Solicitors' Journal* are indexed from 1859 to 1941. Various other journals are also available, and may be found in law libraries and major reference libraries.

A full discussion of these sources would require far more space than is available here. Such a discussion would be superfluous, since the topic has already been covered by a companion volume in the present series:

- BROOKS, BRIAN, & HERBER, MARK. *My ancestor was a lawyer.* Society of Genealogists Enterprises, 2006.

See also:

- WADE, STEPHEN. *Tracing your legal ancestors: a guide for family historians.* Pen & Sword, 2010.
- HOLBORN, GUY. So*urces of biographical information on past lawyers.* British & Irish Association of Law Librarians, 1999.
- How to Trace a Past Solicitor
  www.lawsociety.org.uk/productsandservices/libraryservices/legalresearch guides/view=article.law?PUBLICATIONID=228200

A useful bibliography is provided by:

- Bland, D.S. *A bibliography of the Inns of Court and Chancery.* Selden Society supplementary series **3.** 1965.

I. Medicine

The practice of medicine in England prior to the nineteenth century was disorganised and subject to minimal supervision. Practitioners frequently combined the occupation with a range of other activities. Most had few formal qualifications; it was the services they offered, and their repute, that enabled them to attract patients. Gentlemen practitioners, however, frequently had university degrees, and the biographical dictionaries of Oxford and Cambridge alumni listed above[238] should be consulted for them. In addition, over 2,500 English-speaking students are listed in:

- SMITH, ROBERT WILLIAM. *English speaking students of medicine at the University of Leyden.* Edinburgh,: Oliver & Boyd, 1932.

The medical profession was regarded as providing respectable occupations for younger sons of the gentry. In Bath (Somerset), the high status of the profession was marked by the fact that a surgeon could charge £262 for taking on an apprentice, an apothecary could charge £100.[239] A select few physicians were knights. Such a one was Sir Theodore Mayerne. According to Sir Henry Slingsby, whose wife consulted Mayerne, he 'was rich, and the Kings physitian, and a Knight, which made him more costly to deal with all'[240]. Slingsby did not add that Mayerne was a Huguenot, and had previously been *médecin ordinaire* to Henry IV, the French king.

Most gentlemen who joined the profession would have been either physicians or surgeons, and would probably have been members of their professional organisations. The Royal College of Physicians of London **www.rcplondon.ac.uk/resources/ library/for-historians-and-researchers** was founded in 1518, under the presidency of Thomas Linacre, the King's physician. and claimed a monopoly of the trade of medicine in England, although in practice that monopoly could not be enforced. In 1703, the House of Lords held it to be against the public interest. Its library holds records of its members, that is, its fellows and licentiates, since its beginnings. Biographies of them have been published:

- MUNK, WILLIAM. *The roll of the Royal College of Physicians of London, comprising biographical sketches of all the eminent physicians whose names are recorded in the annals from ... 1518 to ... 1825.* 2nd ed. 3 vols. Harrison & Sons, 1878. This is continued in:
- BROWN, G.H. *Lives of the fellows of the Royal College of Physicians of London 1826-1955.* The College, 1955.

See also:

- Munk's Roll
  http://munksroll.rcplondon.ac.uk

The term 'physician' was usually used to describe a person who diagnosed internal disorders, although some practitioners also carried out surgery and/or dispensed medicines. The latter were usually regarded as separate professions. Surgeons conducted surgery under the supervision of physicians. In 1540, they joined with the barbers to form the Barber Surgeon Company of London. Its members and apprenticeship records, together with registers of certificates issued to persons intending to serve as naval surgeons, are held by Guildhall Library. Some of these records are also held on microform by the Family History Library **www.familysearch.org**.

The Company split in 1745, with the surgeons becoming a separate company, which was re-founded as the Royal College of Surgeons of England in 1800. Its library **www.rcseng.ac.uk/library/using-the-library/historical-research/family-research** holds some resources for family historians, including admission registers, 1745-96. Some records are available on microfilm at Guildhall Library, and at the Family History Library. For the lives of its fellows, see:

- Plarr's Lives of the Fellows Online
  http://livesonline.rcseng.ac.uk
  This is incomplete as yet, and it may be necessary to resort to the printed version:
- PLARR, VICTOR GUSTAVE. *Plarr's lives of the fellows of the Royal College of Surgeons of England.*, rev. Sir Darcy Power, Walter George Spencer, & George Ernest Gask. 2 vols. Wright & Sons for the Royal College of Surgeons, 1930. Continued to 2002 in several further volumes.

Apothecaries were responsible for dispensing medicine. In London, they formed a separate section of the Grocers Company, until they separated in 1617, and the Society of Apothecaries was established. Its apprenticeship and membership records are now in Guildhall Library (see below). Its early apprenticeship registers are abstracted in:

- WALLIS, PATRICK. *London livery company apprenticeship registers, vol.32. Apothecaries Company 1617-1669*. Society of Genealogists, 2000. This is also available as part of a pay-per-view database at **www.origins.net/help/aboutbolonapps.aspx**

Other archives are still held by the Company:

- The Worshipful Company of Apothecaries of London **www.apothecaries.org/index.php?page=2**

Physicians and surgeons required a licence to practise from their diocesan bishop, in accordance with a 1511 Act of Parliament. Registers and other records of licences issued frequently survive in diocesan archives. These are likely to give the name of the licensee, his parish, the date of issue, and the fee paid. Applicants were usually expected to produce testimonials, frequently from other medical professionals, but formal qualifications were not required. Where testimonials survive, they can be very useful. For licences issued by the Archbishop in respect of his Province, see:

- Lambeth Palace Library Research Guide: Medical Licences issued by the Archbishop of Canterbury, 1535-1775 **www.lambethpalacelibrary.org/files/Medical_Licences.pdf**

A number of diocesan collections of medical licences are in print. See, for example:

- BLOOM, J. HARVEY, & JAMES, R. RUTSON. *Medical practitioners in the Diocese of London under the act of 3 Henry VIII, c.II: an annotated list, 1529-1725*. Cambridge University Press, 1935.

Many gentlemen served as officers in the Army's medical services. They are listed in:

- PETERKIN, A., JOHNSTON, WILLIAM, & DREW, ROBERT, SIR. *Commissioned officers in the medical services of the British Army, 1660-1960*. 2 vols. Wellcome Historical Medical Library, 1968.

For officers in the medical service of the East Indian Company army, see:

- DODWELL, EDWARD, & MILES, JAMES S. *An alphabetical list of the medical officers of the Indian Army 1764-1838, with the dates of their respective appointment, promotion, retirement, resignation, or death, whether in India or in Europe, from the year 1764 to the year 1838.* Longman, Orme, Brown, 1839.
- CRAWFORD, D. G. *Roll of the Indian Medical Service, 1615-1930.* Calcutta: Thacker, 1930. Reprinted London Stamp Exchange, 1986.

A full discussion of sources for tracing medical ancestors cannot be given here. For more detailed guidance, consult:

- HIGGS, MICHELLE. *Tracing your medical ancestors: a guide for family historians.* PEN & SWORD, 2011.

See also:

- BOURNE, SUSAN, & CHICKEN, ANDREW H. *Records of the medical profession: a practical guide for the family historian.* The authors, 1994.
- Was Your Ancestor a Doctor?
  http://user.itl.net/~glen/doctors.html
- Doctors: Physicians, Surgeons, Dentists and Apothecaries in England
  https://wiki.familysearch.org/en/Doctors:_Physicians,_Surgeons,_Dentists _and_Apothecaries_in_England

A useful bibliography is provided by:

- THORNTON, JOHN L. *A select bibliography of medical biography.* 2nd ed. Library Association, 1970.

A number of biographical dictionaries are available:

- TALBOT, C. H., & HAMMOND, E.A. *The medical practitioners in medieval England: a biographical register.* Wellcome Historical Medical Library, 1965.
- RAACH, JOHN H. *A directory of English country physicians, 1603-1643.* Dawsons of Pall Mall, 1962.
- WALLIS, J., & WALLIS, R.V. *Eighteenth century medics (subscriptions, licences, apprenticeships).* 2nd ed. Newcastle upon Tyne: Project for Historical Biobibliography, 1988.

London's Wellcome Library is the leading institution for the study of medical history. It holds a variety of resources relevant to family history. See:

- Biographical and Family History Resources in the Wellcome Library
  http://library.wellcome.ac.uk/assets/wtx049847.pdf

For sources at Guildhall Library, visit:

- Sources for tracing Apothecaries, Surgeons, Physicians, and other Medical Practitioners at Guildhall Library
  www.history.ac.uk/gh/apoths.htm

J. Apprenticeship and Trade

The wealthier your father was, the less likely you were to go into trade. Nevertheless, the younger sons of many gentlemen did serve apprenticeships, and became tradesmen. Of course, if their parents could afford to pay a higher premium, they entered high status trades. Many entered the employment of the East India Company. Others became city merchants or bankers.

In order to qualify for such careers, it was necessary to enter an apprenticeship with a qualified master. Masters in high status trades could demand a premium of as much as £1000 or more to take on a gentleman's son. It must be borne in mind that they could lose substantial sums through their apprentice's carelessness or mistakes. The apprentice would agree to serve his master for seven years, and to obey his lawful commands. He would lodge in his master's house, and would be provided with food and clothing at his master's expense. The master would accept responsibility for teaching the apprentice his trade.

An apprenticeship was not generally regarded as ideal for a gentleman's son. From his family's point of view, it was frequently regarded as demeaning. From a master's point of view, although such an apprentice would bring a substantial premium, he might take a dim view of accepting orders from a mere tradesman - or taking any punishment that might be meted out. A gentleman's son might be much harder to teach than an apprentice of lower status. Nevertheless, the records show that many gentlemen did have their sons apprenticed. The attitude of Percival Willoughby, who pressed his father to apprentice him to a physician, was a sensible one: he saw the indebtedness of both his father and his brothers, and decided that, as a physician, 'he believed that he could never stand in need of them, but he questioned not but they would stand in need of him'[241]. The story of Dick Whittington (c.1350-1423)[242] and his apprenticeship has become legendary. He was the younger son of a minor Gloucestershire gentleman, Sir William Whittington of Pauntley, and was apprenticed to a London mercer. He famously married his master's daughter, and became Lord Mayor of London. His career showed what was possible: the fifteenth century equivalent of the American dream. Others in similar situations sometimes purchased an estate and established new lines of county gentry. Our Dick, sadly, had no children to inherit his wealth. According to Harrison, writing in the sixteenth century, merchants 'often change estates with gentlemen, as gentlemen do with them; by a mutual conversion of the one into the other'[243].

The basic document recording apprenticeship is the indenture. These were completed in duplicate, one copy for the master, one for the apprentice (or his father). The indenture identifies the respective parties, naming parents and their residences, and setting out the duties of both master and apprentice.

Unfortunately, private indentures did not have to be deposited in any official repository. Nevertheless, many can be found amongst borough archives, in the records of guilds and (in London) livery companies, and amongst family papers. These can sometimes be traced through A2A **www.nationalarchives.gov.uk/a2a**. It is also worth asking relevant record offices whether they hold any collections of indentures.

If apprentice indentures cannot be traced, it may still be possible to discover some of their contents. Most boroughs, and some guilds, kept registers of apprentices which provide abstracts of the information contained in indentures. For London, the registers of over 40 livery companies have been indexed in:

- WEBB, CLIFFORD REGINALD. *London livery company apprenticeship registers: abstracts and indexes.* 44+ vols to date. Society of Genealogists, 1996- .

These registers, together with a number of others, are also abstracted online:

- London Apprenticeship Abstracts 1552-1850
  www.londonorigins.com/help/popup-aboutbo-lonapps.htm

A number of borough apprenticeship registers have been published by record societies. See for example:

- BARLOW, JILL, ed. *A Calendar of the registers of the apprentices of the City of Gloucester, 1595-1700.* Gloucestershire record series **14**. Bristol & Gloucestershire Archaeological Society, 2001.
- WILLIS, ARTHUR JOHN, & MERSON, ALLAN LESLIE, eds. *A calendar of Southampton apprenticeship registers, 1609-1740.* Southampton Records series **12**. 1968.

Information drawn from apprenticeship indentures can also be found in the Stamp Duty Registers, now in TNA (class IR 1). The Stamp Duty Act 1709 imposed a duty of 6d. in the pound on all apprenticeship indentures with a premium of under £50, and 1/- in the pound on indentures where premiums were above this sum. The duty was in force from 1710 until 1804, although the final payments were not made until 1811. The information in the registers was based on the information provided by indentures, and recorded the name and address of the master, the name of the apprentice (and, until 1752, details of his father), the date of the indentures, the date duty was paid, the starting date of the apprenticeship, details of any transfer or assignment of the indentures, and the premium paid. After 1760, the amount of information given decreases, and is sometimes minimal. A digitised database of these registers is now available at:

- UK Registers of Duties Paid for Apprentices Indentures 1710-1811
  http://search.ancestry.co.uk/search/db.aspx?dbid=1851

A database of the Society of Genealogists' abstracts from these registers is also available at:

- Apprentices of Great Britain 1710-1774
  www.findmypast.co.uk/search/apprentices-of-great-britain

For a more detailed guide to these records, and to a wide variety of other apprenticeship records, consult:

- RAYMOND, STUART A. *My ancestor was an apprentice: how can I find out more about him?* Society of Genealogists Enterprises, 2010.

It may also be useful to consult:

- Apprenticeship Records
  www.nationalarchives.gov.uk/records/research-guides/apprenticeship-records.htm

K. East India Company

The East India Company was established in 1600 to trade with the 'Indies'. In the second half of the eighteenth century, this organization was transformed from a mere trading company into a major territorial power in India. Many gentry held shares in the Company, or served as directors. Their younger sons became servants of the Company, and many returned to England as nabobs. Sir John Call, for example, entered the Company's service as a writer, and was able to return to England in 1770 with an ample fortune, which he was able to use to establish himself on a country estate at Whiteford (Cornwall), subsequently becoming an MP and a baronet. Another example is provided by Richard Barwell, the second son of one of the Company's directors. His connection enabled him to join the Company as a writer in 1758. He made his fortune, and returned to England in 1780. In 1781, he was able to purchase Stansted House (Sussex) from the Earl of Halifax, for the huge sum of £102,500[244].

The records of the East India Company are now in the British Library. They include a wide range of sources, including extensive registers of baptisms, marriages, and burials, wills, and a wide range of other sources. Some of these (including the registers) are indexed in the Biographical Index, which includes 300,000 entries. For details, visit:

- British Library: India Office Records; Family History Sources
  www.bl.uk/reshelp/findhelpregion/asia/india/indiaofficerecordsfamilyhistory/familyresearch.html

In 1806, the Company opened a college to train its writers. Students were aged between 16 and 18, and were nominated by the directors of the Company. College records (together with some appointment papers dating back to 1749) are described in:

- FARRINGTON, ANTHONY. *The records of the East India College, Haileybury, and other institutions.* HMSO, 1976.

Appointments to the service of the Company are recorded in the minutes of the Court of Directors and Court of Proprietors, 1599-1858. Another source of information on new appointments are the arrival and departure notices published in newspapers, almanacs, directories, etc., in India. Some of these are indexed at:

- Arrival and Departure Notices
  http://wiki.fibis.org/index.php?title=Arrival_and_Departure_notices

Many memorial inscriptions have been transcribed and published by:

- British Association for Cemeteries in South Asia
  www.bacsa.org.uk

For a database listing over 700,000 names, derived from a range of different sources, visit the website of the:

- Families in British India Society
www.new.fibis.org
This website also includes the 'Fibiwiki' page, which offers much useful information.

The most comprehensive guide to Company records is:

- JOLLY, EMMA. *Tracing your British Indian ancestors: a guide for family historians.* Pen & Sword, 2012.

See also:

- MOIR, MARTIN. *A general guide to the India Office records.* British Library, 1988.
- BAXTER, IAN A. *Baxter's guide:* A *brief guide to biographical sources.* 3rd ed. Families in British India Society, 2004.
- BAILEY, PETER A. *Researching ancestors in the East India Company armies.* Families in British India Society, 2006.

For the holdings of the Society of Genealogists, see:

- TAYLOR, NEVILLE C. *Sources for Anglo-Indian genealogy in the library of the Society of genealogists.* The Society, 1990.

L. Annuitants

Nabobs - and others - did not necessarily invest all their wealth in property. Many purchased annuities. These provided a useful means to support widows and younger sons; census returns have many references to annuitants. Many annuitants received their annuities from family settlements. It was, however, possible to purchase annuities from the state. State annuities commenced in the 1690s. They gave a fixed annual return on the capital invested. Tontines were variable annuities; investors paid a fixed sum into the tontine fund, on which the government paid interest. As investors died off, the interest on their capital was divided amongst surviving investors, so that the longest surviving annuitant received considerable sums.

The records of governmental annuities and tontines are in TNA, classes NDO1-3. Full details are given in:

- LEESON, F. L. *A guide to the records of British state tontines and life annuities of the seventeenth and eighteenth centuries.* Pinhorn Handbooks, 1968.
- LEESON, FRANCIS. *Index to the British state tontine 1776 and annuities 1745-1779* Microfiche. Society of Genealogists, 1994.

CHAPTER TWELVE
Conclusion

The gentry have recently been described as 'the most knowable people that have ever lived'[245]. They left behind them a huge mass of documentation, which is now in record offices throughout the country - and indeed in some overseas record offices. The papers of the Grenville family, for example, are now in the Huntington Library in San Marino, California[246]. This mountain of paper makes it possible to reconstruct the stories of gentry lives in much more detail than is possible for the ordinary run of humanity. Consequently, the family historian who has gentry ancestors is likely to have a great deal of research to undertake.

Much of that research will concern landed property. Possession of land was perhaps the most distinguishing characteristic of the gentry. It was the basis of their position in society, and of their power. The story of the descent of land through successive generations is likely to be central to the family historian's story. The country houses which the gentry built on their land, and which can frequently still be visited today, provided the theatre in which they lived their lives. Some still do - but relatively few.

In the nineteenth century, it was not so much that the gentry declined, as that industrialists and commercial interests rose. The gentry way of life - going on the Grand Tour, attending Quarter Sessions and (perhaps) Parliament, the Season in London, running a landed estate, the hunting and shooting,

continued. That was encapsulated in the biography of Philip Pusey[247], the grandson of a Viscount on his father's side and of an Earl on his mother's side, although he himself held no title. He attended Eton and Oxford (although, like many other eldest sons, he did not take a degree). He went on the Grand Tour, and was captured by Spanish revolutionaries who mistook him for a soldier of the Cortes. He married the sister of Lord Porchester, and took her to Rome, where they lived for six years. But when he inherited the family estate in 1828, he returned home. He took on the management of his home farm himself, and thus acquired much practical experience in agriculture, which he put to use in founding the Royal Agricultural Society, and in his House of Commons career. He was also a keen sportsman.

The real decline of the country gentleman began with the deaths of so many young gentlemen in the First World War. It may be hyperbole to say that an entire generation was wiped out, but that is what it felt like to contemporaries. Recovery could, perhaps, have taken place in time - had it not been for the impact of death duties. Almost every guide book to a National Trust or English Heritage property recounts the fact that the last gentry owners suffered from death duties, and could not afford the continuing costs involved in looking after large historic properties. They either had to sell up, or to donate their property to the current custodians. In Devon, the Acland family in the 1940s knew that death duties would probably destroy their estate within a couple of generations, and could not afford the cost of maintaining their house at Killerton: it was thought that 8 servants were needed to do so. The situation was complicated by the fact that Richard Acland, the head of the family, was the war-time leader of the Common Wealth Party, which advocated common ownership of the land - a view which he thought to be incompatible with ownership of a large estate. The Aclands, perhaps, symbolise the increasing democratisation of society which led to the gentry being reduced to anachronism. The solution adopted by Richard Acland was simple: 17,000 acres was donated to the National Trust in 1943[248].

Thus ended gentry domination in this part of East Devon. All that was left was for the history of the family to be written[249]. Most gentry families experienced similar decline; they are waiting for you to write their history.

1. For full listings of directories, see NORTON, JANE E. *Guide to the national and provincial directories of England and Wales, excluding London, published before 1856.* Royal Historical Society guides and handbooks 5. 1950; SHAW, GARETH, & TIPPER, ALISON. *British directories: a bibliography and guide to directories published in England and Wales (1850-1950) and Scotland (1773-1950).* 2nd ed. Mansell Publishing, 1997.

2. Cited by LLOYD, H.A. *The gentry of South-West Wales 1540-1640.* University of Wales Press, 1968, p.17.

3. HARRISON, WILLIAM. *The description of England,* ed. Georges Edelen. Folger Shakespeare Library, 1994, p.113-114.

4. Cited by KEEN, MAURICE. *Origins of the English gentleman.* Tempus, 2002, p.22.

5. Ibid, p.96.

6. HEAL & HOLMES, *The Gentry in England and Wales, 1500-1700.* Stanford University Press, 1994, p.7.

7. **http://princehamlet.com/burghley.html**

8. Cited by JOHNSON, JOAN. *The Gloucestershire gentry.* Alan Sutton, 1989, p.31.

9. Ibid, p.134. The contrary view - that a man of law could not be a gentleman - is quoted in DENHOLM- YOUNG, N. *The country gentry in the fourteenth century.* Clarendon Press, 1969, p.130

10. HEAL & HOLMES, op cit, p.179.

11. JACOB, GILES. *A new law dictionary* ... 1743, cf. 'Age'. This book is digitised at **www.archive.org**.

12. BELL, H. E. *An introduction to the history and records of the Court of Wards & Liveries.* Cambridge University Press, 1953, p.126.

13. JENKINS, PHILIP. *The making of a ruling class: the Glamorgan gentry 1640-1790.* Cambridge University Press, 1983, p.55.

14. **http://privatewww.essex.ac.uk/~alan/family/N-Money.html#1825**. On domestic servants, see HORN, PAMELA. *My ancestor was in service: a guide to sources for family historians.* Society of Genealogists, 2009.

15. WILSON, THOMAS. 'The State of England anno dom 1600', ed. F. J. Fisher. *Camden miscellany* **16**. Camden 3rd series **52**. Royal Historical Society, 1936, pp.23-24.

16. CLIFFE, J. T. *The Yorkshire gentry from the reformation to the civil war.* Athlone Press, 1968, p.6.

17. CLIFFE, op cit, p.7.

18. CLIFFE, op cit, p.111.

19. WILSON, op cit, p.23.

20. DRAKE, DAPHNE. 'Members of Parliament for Barnstaple', *Devonshire Association ... transactions*, **72**, 1940, p.262.

21. KEEN, MAURICE. *The origins of the English gentleman.* Chatto, 2002, p.104.

22. See below, pp.33-38

23. WAGNER, ANTHONY. *English genealogy.* 3rd ed. Phillimore, 1983, p.124.

24. STONE, LAWRENCE, & STONE, JEANNE C. FAWTIER. *An open elite? England 1540-1880.* Clarendon Press, 1984, p.11.

25. MINGAY, op cit, p.7.

26. NICOLSON, ADAM. *Gentry. Six hundred years of a peculiarly English class.* Harper Press, 2011, p.x.

27. HOSKINS, W. G. 'The re-building of rural England, 1570-1640', *Past and present,* 4, 1953, pp.44-59; MACHIN, R. 'The great rebuilding: a reassessment', *Past and present,* 77, 1977, pp.33-56. PLATT, COLIN. *The Great Rebuildings of Tudor and Stuart England: revolutions in architectural taste.* UCL Press, 1994; STONE, op cit, p.386.

28. CLIFFE, op cit, pp.102-103.

29. CLIFFE, op cit, p.15.

30. STONE, op cit, pp.102-104.

31. CLIFFE, op cit, pp.95-96.

32. Ibid, p.97.

33. HEAL & HOLMES, op cit, p.109.

34. TUSSER, THOMAS. *Five hundred points of good husbandry.* Oxford University Press, 1984,

35. The 1573 edition incorporated some poems published earlier.

36. Cited by HEAL & HOLMES, op cit, p.102.

37. JENKINS, PHILIP. *The making of a ruling class: the Glamorgan gentry 1640-1790.* Cambridge University Press, 1983, p.45 and 61.

38. RAMSAY, G. D. *The Wiltshire woollen industry in the sixteenth and seventeenth centuries.* 2nd ed. Frank Cass, 1965, pp.31-37.

39. STONE, op cit, p.12.

40. MINGAY, op cit, p59.

41. STONE, op cit, p.160 and 180.

42. Cited by HEAL & HOLMES, op cit, p.104.

43. TUSSER, op cit, p.20.

44. Cited by HEAL & HOLMES, op cit, p.59.

45. TROLLOPE, ANTHONY. *The last chronicle of Barsetshire.* 1867.
www.gutenberg.org/files/3045/3045-h/3045-h.htm

46. MINGAY, op cit, pp.4-5.

47. CLIFFE, op cit, p.342.

48. STONE, L. 'The inflation of honours, 1558-1641', *Past & present,* **14**, 1958, pp.45-70.

49. AYLMER, G. E. *The King's servants: the civil service of Charles I, 1625-1642.* Routledge & Kegan Paul, 1961, p.260.

50. COSS, PETER. *The origins of the English gentry.* Cambridge University Press, 2003, p.6.

51. JENKINS. op cit, p.29 and 40.

52. CLIFFE, op cit, p.124.

53. MINGAY, op cit, p.48.

54. CLIFFE, op cit, p.137.

55. ROWSE, A. L. *Tudor Cornwall.* New ed. Macmillan, 1969, pp.85-86.

56. CORNWALL, JULIAN. *Revolt of the peasantry 1549.* Routledge & Kegan Paul, 1974, p.231.

57. NICOLSON, ADAM. *Gentry: six hundred years of a peculiarly English class.* Harper, 2011, p.xvii.

58. RAMSAY, op cit, pp.45-46.

59. RAMSAY, op cit, p.42.

60. FINCH, MARY E. *The wealth of five Northamptonshire families 1540-1640.* Northamptonshire Record Society 19. 1956, pp.38-65. See also **www.althorp.com/estate_family_history.php**

61. MINGAY, op cit, p.6.

62. STONE, op cit, pp.212-221.

63. ELTON, H. R. *England under the Tudors.* Methuen & Co., 1955, p.258.

64. Quoted by MINGAY, op cit, p.7.

65. COSS, op cit, p.15.

66. CLIFFE, op cit, p.231.

67. CLIFFE, op cit, p.200.

68. See CLIFFE, op cit.

69. SMITH, THOMAS. *De Republica Anglorum: a discourse on the Commonwealth of England.,* ed L. Alston. Cambridge University Press, 1906, p.86 and 88. Cited by ROWSE, op cit, p.83.

70. CLIFFE, op cit, p.233.

71. GLASSEY, LIONEL K. J. *Politics and the appointment of Justices of the Peace, 1675-1720.* Oxford University Press, 1979, p.15.

72. Cited by HEAL & HOLMES, op cit, p.167.

73. STONE, op cit, pp.270-271.

74. KOLBERT, J. M. *The Sneyds, squires of Keele.* University of Keele, 1976, chapter 6 (unpaginated).

75. WINTER, J. M. *The Great War and the British people.* 2nd ed. Palgrave Macmillan, 2003, p.97.

76. See above, p.4.

77. KEEN, MAURICE. *Origins of the gentleman.* Tempus, 2002, p.21.

78. JONES, J. GWYNFOR. *The Welsh gentry: images of status, honour and authority.* University of Wales Press, 1998, p.117.

79. STONE, L. *The crisis of the aristocracy, 1558-1641.* Abridged ed. Oxford University Press, 1965, p.16.

80. KEEN, MAURICE. *Origins of the English gentleman.* Tempus, 2002, p.98.

81. WALES, T. C., & HARTLEY, C. P., eds. *The visitation of London begun in 1687.* Part 1. Publications of the Harleian Society, new series 16. 2004, p.xxxv.

82. Quoted by SQUIBB, G. D. *Visitation pedigrees and the genealogist.* 2nd ed. Pinhorns, 1978, p.6.

83. WALES & HARTLEY, op cit, p.xliii.

84. KEEN, op cit, p.20.

85. SQUIBB, op cit, p.4.

86. See, for example, SYMONDS, RICHARD. *Diary of the marches of the Royal Army during the great civil war* , ed. Charles Edward Long. Camden Society **74**. 1859.

87. WALES & HARTLEY, op cit, pp.153-154.

88. See SQUIBB, op cit, pp.37-39, for some criticisms of this work, and for details of other publications where disclaimers have been published.

89. SQUIBB, op cit, contains a detailed review of the accuracy of visitation pedigrees.

90. For a detailed list of their contents, see the work by the present author listed on p.21.

91. COSS, op cit. p.69.

92. I owe this point to Ellie Pridgeon, formerly librarian of the Wiltshire Archaeological & Natural History Society.

93. A useful list of both printed and manuscript transcriptions made before 1861 can be found in SIMS, RICHARD. A *manual for the genealogist, topographer, antiquary, and legal professor.* 2nd ed. John Russell Smith, 1861, pp.286-294.

94. COSS, op cit, p.139.

95. HEAL & HOLMES, op cit, p.56.

96. I am grateful to David Oates for providing these details, and for the photograph. See SUMMERS, PETER, & TITTERTON, JOHN. *Hatchments in Britain,* vol 7. Phillimore, 1988. pp 33-34.

97. SIMS, RICHARD. A *manual for the genealogist, topographer, antiquary, and legal professor.* 2nd ed. John Russell Smith, 1861, pp.279-280.

98. STONE, op cit, p.70. This chapter draws heavily on Stone's chapter 4.

99. SCOTT, H. S., ed. *The journal of Sir Roger Wilbraham, Solicitor-General in Ireland and Master of Requests, for the years 1598-1616 ... .* Camden miscellany **10**. Camden Society 3rd series, **4**. 1902, p.22.

100. JENKINS, op cit, p.67.

101. STONE, op cit, p.72.

102. BONFIELD, LLOYD. *Marriage settlements, 1601-1740.* Cambridge University Press, 1983, pp.86-91.

103. MINGAY, op cit, p.110.

104. SHEPPARD, F., & BELCHER, V. 'The deeds registries of Yorkshire and Middlesex', *Journal of the Society of Archivists*, **6**(5), 1980, pp.274-286.

105. ENGLISH, BARBARA, & SAVILLE, JOHN. *Strict settlement: a guide for historians.* University of Hull Press, 1983, p.18.

106. The following paragraphs depend heavily on English & Saville, op cit, pp.17-30.

107. See below, p.59.

108. ENGLISH & SAVILLE, op cit, p.48.

109. THORNE, R. G., ed. *The Commons 1790-1820, vol.3. Members A-F.* Secker & Warburg, 1986, pp.135-136.

110. ENGLISH & SAVILLE, op cit, p.50.

111. HEAL & HOLMES, op cit, p.86.

112. HEAL & HOLMES, op cit, p.61.

113. For parish registers, consult RAYMOND, STUART A. *Parish registers: a history & guide.* Family History Partnership, 2009.

114. Society of Genealogists Documents Collection: deeds relating to Thomas Brockhurst Barclay.

115. STONE, op cit, p.142.

116. STONE, op cit, p.132.

117. STONE, op cit, p.136.

118. STONE, op cit, p.128.

119. STONE, op cit, p.139.

120. DENHOLM-YOUNG, N. *The country gentry in the fourteenth century.* Clarendon Press, 1969, p.130.

121. See above, p.51.

122. HARVEY, ROBIN & BARBARA. *Winsley from Cecilia to Victoria.* Hobnob Press, 2007, p.42.

123. See pp.84-85.

124. For a full list, see RAYMOND, S.A. *The wills of our ancestors: the family and local historian's guide to probate records.* Pen & Sword, 2012.

125. JENKINS, op cit, p.69.

126. RAVENHILL, MARY, & ROSE, MARGERY M., eds. *The Acland family: maps and surveys 1720-1840.* Devon & Cornwall Record Society 49. 2006, p.72.

127. Cited by JONES, J. GWYNFOR. T*he Welsh gentry 1536-1640: images of status, honour, and authority.* University of Wales Press, 1998, p.21.

128. For lawyers, see below, pp.128-132.

129. CLIFFE, op cit, p.137.

130. In HEY, DAVID. *The Oxford companion to local and family history.* 2nd ed. 2008, p.218. Much of what follows is based on Hoyle's article.

131. **www.court-of-chivalry.bham.ac.uk/objectives.htm**

132. For common recoveries, see p.51 above; for feet of fines, p.59.

133. Cited by CLIFFE, J. T. *The puritan gentry: the great puritan families of early Stuart England.* Routledge & Kegan Paul, 1984, p.105.

134. GUY, JOHN. *The Tudors: a very short introduction.* Oxford University Press, 1984, p.83.

135. Cited by HEAL & HOLMES, op cit, p.157.

136. For the database of this class, see above, p.83.

137. See below, p.121.

138. DENHOLM-YOUNG, N. *The country gentleman in the fourteenth century ...* Oxford University Press, 1969, p.47.

139. BELL, H. E. *An introduction to the history and records of the Court of Wards & Liveries.* Cambridge University Press, 1953, p.2.

140. Ibid, p.57.

141. For these, see above, pp.59-60.

142. BELL, op cit, p.116.

143. HEAL & HOLMES, op cit, p.144.

144. CLIFFE, op cit, p.130.

145. For these officials, see below, p.109.

146. CLIFFE, op cit, p.131.

147. WOLFFE, MARY. *Gentry leaders in peace and war: the gentry governors of Devon in the early seventeenth century.* University of Exeter Press, 1997, p.87.

148. CLIFFE, op cit, p.246.

149. The numbers of nonconformist recusants increased after 1660.

150. NICOLSON, ADAM. *Gentry: six hundred years of a peculiarly English class.* Harper Press, 2011, p.67.

151. HEAL & HOLMES, op cit, p.148.

152. HEAL & HOLMES, op cit, p.146.

153. HEAL & HOLMES, op cit, p.147.

154. *Oxford dictionary of national biography* **www.oxforddnb.com.**

155. *Oxford dictionary of national biography* **www.oxforddnb.com.**

156. CLIFFE, op cit, pp.208-209.

157. CLIFFE, op cit, p.213.

158. RAYMOND, S. A. 'The Glamorgan Arraymen, 1642-45', *Morgannwg* **24**, 1980, pp.16-18.

159. HEAL & HOLMES, op cit, p.151.

160. GREEN, M. A. E., ed. *Calendar of the Committee for Compounding ... .* 1889-93, vol.2, pp.1033-1034.

161. Cited by HEAL & HOLMES, op cit, p.220.

162. Cited by HEAL & HOLMES, op cit, p.154.

163. See below, p.121.

164. See above, p.84.

165. For a detailed discussion of 'the gentry as royal tax collectors', see WOLFFE, MARY. *Gentry leaders in peace and war: the gentry governors of Devon in the early seventeenth century..* University of Exeter Press, 1997, pp.69-89.

166. COSS, op cit, p.167.

167. COSS, op cit, passim.

168. JOHNSON, JOAN. *The Gloucestershire gentry.* Alan Sutton, 1989, p140.

169. RAMSAY, G.D., op cit, p.47.

170. CLIFFE, op cit, p.255.

171. Cited by HEAL & HOLMES, op cit, p.172.

172. ROWSE, A. L. *Sir Richard Grenville of the Revenge.* Jonathan Cape, 1937, p.144. See above, pp.91-92, for the fate of two of the men he arrested, ie Francis Tregian and Cuthbert Mayne.

173. STONE, op cit, p.272.

174. BOYNTON, LINDSAY. *The Elizabethan militia 1558-1638.* David & Charles, 1971, p.9.

175. CLIFFE, op cit, p.232.

176. BOYNTON, op cit, p.7.

177. BOYNTON, op cit, p.101.

178. See below, pp.120-121.

179. Northamptonshire Record Office, FH 133. For discussion of Arraymen's activities, see RAYMOND, S. A. 'The Glamorganshire Arraymen 1642-45', *Morgannwg* **24**, 1980, pp.9-30.

180. For a Parliamentary county committee order book, see: PENNINGTON, D. H., & ROOTS, I. A., eds. *The Committee at Stafford 1643-1645: the order book of the Staffordshire County Committee.* Staffordshire Record Society 4th series, **1**. 1956.

181. See above, pp.87-90.

182. BELL, H. E. *An introduction to the history and records of the Court of Wards & Liveries.* Cambridge University Press, 1953, p.41.

183. Ibid, p.39.

184. HEAL & HOLMES, p.259.

185. STONE, op cit, p.27.

186. STONE, op cit, p.262-263.

187. HEAL & HOLMES, op cit, p.264.

188. For a discussion of the accuracy of matriculation registers, see STONE, L. 'The size and composition of the Oxford student body', in STONE, L., ed. *The university in society.* 1974, vol.1. Princeton University Press, 1974, pp.3-110.

189. CLIFFE, op cit, p.172, 194, and 196-197.

190. Others can be identified in the bibliographies listed on p.93.

191. **http://princehamlet.com/burghley.html**

192. CLIFFE, op cit, p.76-77.

193. *Anglia Notitia,* 1669, p.486-487, cited by STONE, op cit, p.20.

194. BAMFORD, F., ed. *A royalist's notebook: the commonplace book of Sir John Oglander of Nunwell, 1622-1652.* Constable, 1936, p.75.

195. CLIFFE, op cit, p.85 and 94.

196. WALES & HARTLEY, op cit, p.xxvi.

197. STONE, op cit, p.196.

198. STONE, op cit, p.210.

199. HEAL & HOLMES, op cit, p.87-88.

200. WILSON, op cit, p.24.

201. GRASSBY, R. B. 'Social mobility and business enterprise in seventeenth-century London', in PENNINGTON, D., & THOMAS, K., eds. *Puritans and revolutionaries: essays in seventeenth-century history presented to Christopher Hill.* Clarendon Press, 1978, p.356.

202. Cited by CLIFFE, J. T. *The puritan gentry: the great puritan families of early Stuart England.* Routledge & Kegan Paul, 1984, p.108.

203. STONE, op cit, pp.234-235.

204. CLIFFE, op cit, p.92.

205. THOMAS, JAMES H. 'The Isle of Wight and the East India Company 1700-1840', *Local historian* **20**(1), 2000, p.5.

206. CLIFFE, op cit, p.92.

207. *Oxford Dictionary of national biography* **www.oxforddnb.com**

208. HEAL & HOLMES, op cit, pp.128-129.

209. *Oxford dictionary of national biography* **www.oxforddnb.com**; HEAL & HOLMES, op cit, p.131.

210. AYLMER, G. E. *The King's servants: the civil service of Charles I, 1625-1642.* Routledge & Kegan Paul, 1961, p.263, 278, and 325.

211. HUTCHINSON, LUCY. *Memoirs of Colonel Hutchinson,* ed. Julius Hutchinson. Rev. ed. Everyman's Library, 1968, p.7.

212. AYLMER, op cit, p.85.

213. JENKINS, op cit, p.120.

214. AYLMER, op cit, p.229.

215. AYLMER, op cit, p.107.

216. AYLMER, op cit, p.109.

217. AYLMER, op cit, p.339.

218. CLIFFE, op cit, p.88.

219. CLIFFE, op cit, p.89.

220. See above, pp.120-121.

221. WINTER, J. M. *The Great War and the British people.* Palgrave, 2003, p.86.

222. O'DAY, ROSEMARY. *The English clergy: the emergence and consolidation of a profession, 1558-1642.* Leicester University Press, 1979, p.189.

223. JENKINS, op cit, p.90.

224. DEW, R. *A history of the parish and church of Kilkhampton.* 2nd ed. Wells, Gardner, Darton & Co., 1928, pp.30-31 and 52.

225. STONE, op cit, p.230.

226. JENKINS, op cit, p.224.

227. MINGAY, op cit, p.128; JENKINS, op cit, p.89.

228. For some other useful books, see the bibliographies listed on p.93.

229. HEAL & HOLMES, op cit, p.133.

230. Cited by HEAL & HOLMES, op cit, p.133.

231. JOHNSON, op cit, p.204.

232. See BROOKS, BRIAN, & HERBER, MARK. *My ancestor was a lawyer.* Society of Genealogists, 2008, pp.34-41 for a detailed account of the Inns of Chancery.

233. CLIFFE, op cit, p.87.

234. CLIFFE, op cit, p.86.

235. Nigel Saul, quoted by JOHNSON, JOAN. *The Gloucestershire gentry,* Alan Sutton, 1989, p.23.

236. JENKINS, PHILIP. *The making of a ruling class: the Glamorgan gentry 1640-1790.* Cambridge University Press, 1983, pp.55-66.

237. See above, pp.69-75. For the judicial archives of the House of Lords consult BOND, MAURICE F. *Guide to the records of Parliament.* HMSO, 1971, p.106-126. These are of limited use for tracing lawyers.

238. See p.113.

239. WROUGHTON, JOHN. S*tuart Bath: life in the forgotten city, 1603-1714.* Lansdown Press, 2004, p.119.

240. Cited by CLIFFE, op cit, p.22.

241. Cited by HEAL & HOLMES, op cit, p.88.

242. *Oxford dictionary of national biography* **www.oxforddnb.com**

243. HARRISON, op cit, p.115.

244. See the biographies in the *Oxford dictionary of national biography* **www.oxforddnb.com** (or in its print version)

245. NICOLSON, ADAM. *Gentry: six hundred years of a peculiarly English class.* Harper Press, 2012, p.ix.

246. **www.dukesofbuckingham.org.uk/sources/documents/huntington/stg/stg.htm**

247. THOMPSON, F.M.L. 'Pusey, Philip, 1799-1855', *Oxford dictionary of national biography,* **www.oxforddnb.com/view/article/22911**.

248. ACLAND, ANNE. *Killerton.* National Trust, 1997, pp.29-30. See also Nicolson, op cit, pp.349-384.

249. ACLAND, ANNE. *A Devon family: the story of the Aclands.* Phillimore, 1981.

INDEX

Subject Index

Pedigrees, 16, 17, 19, 20, 21, 28, 29, 31, 32, 33, 34, 35, 36, 37, 49, 50, 115
Pedigrees, Royal, 30
Peerage, 24, 29, 30, 31, 32
Physicians, 92, 132, 133, 134, 135, 136
Poll Books, 99, 100
Poll Tax, 81
Prayer Book Rebellion, 1549, 13, 117
Prerogative Court of Canterbury, 52, 64, 131
Primogeniture, 11, 48, 50, 116
Privy Council registers, 114, 115
Probate, 8, 49, 63, 64, 65
Professionalism, 116
Protestation, 97, 98
Puritanism, 15, 63, 79, 91, 116

Quarter Sessions, 15, 91, 99, 100, 105, 131, 141
Quitclaim, 59

Racing Horses Duty, 85
Recusancy Fines, 81, 90, 91, 92
Recusants, 11, 90, 91, 92, 93, 98, 114, 118
Religious Clauses, 63
Rentals, 57, 58, 59, 66
Return of owners of land, 11, 67, 68
Rolls of Arms, 44
Roman Catholics, 11, 13, 15, 63, 79, 81, 91, 92, 99, 104, 113, 114
Roman Catholics, Clergy, 127
Rootsweb, 22
Royal Agricultural Society, 142
Royal College of Physicians, 132, 133
Royal College of Surgeons, 133
Royal Household, 14, 108, 121, 122
Royalist Composition Papers, 93, 94

Sacrament Certificates, 99
Saddle and Carriage Horses Duty, 85
School Registers, 111, 112
Scriveners, 49, 116, 129, 130
Scriveners' Company, 130
Selden Society, 71, 131
Sequestration Committee, 94
Servants, 4, 5, 12, 57, 63, 119, 142
Settlements, 1, 5, 11, 48, 49, 50, 51, 52, 53, 54, 57, 58, 59, 63, 77, 105, 116, 140
Settlements, Marriage, 47, 52, 53, 54, 55, 77
Sheriffs, 11, 14, 33, 100, 101, 102, 103, 104, 106, 129

Sheriffs' Rolls, 104
Silver Plate Duty, 85
Society of Apothecaries, 134
Society of Genealogists, 20, 29, 72, 85, 100, 112, 130, 138, 140
Solemn League & Covenant, 93, 98
Solicitor's journal, 131
Spelling, 56
Stained Glass, 34
Star Chamber, 69, 70, 74, 75
State Papers Domestic, 94, 95, 120, 121, 123
Status, 3, 4, 5, 6, 7, 8, 12, 19, 33, 39, 47, 52, 57, 69, 102, 105, 116, 132, 136
Stewards, 5, 9, 62, 66, 119, 130
Subsidies, 81, 83, 84, 86, 91
Surgeons, 132, 133, 134, 135, 136
Surgeons, Naval, 133
Surnames, 30, 39, 44, 47, 54, 55
Surnames, Double-Barrelled, 55
Surveys, 57, 58, 59, 62, 66, 89, 109

Taxation, 1, 8, 81, 82, 83, 87, 91
Tenant in Tail, 50, 51
Times, 25
Tithe Maps, 67, 68, 69
Tithes, 67, 68, 69
Title Deeds, 1
Tontines, 140
Topographer & genealogist, 21
Trade, 8, 10, 102, 116, 136
Treason, 51, 95

Universities, 3, 15, 16, 111, 112, 113, 124, 132
University Registers, 111, 112

Valuation Office, 67, 68, 69
View of Frankpledge, 62
Visitations, Heraldic, 8, 16, 28, 33, 34, 35, 36, 37, 115
Vow and Covenant, 1643, 98

Wall Memorials, 42
Wardship, 11, 81, 87, 88, 90, 109, 118
Websites, 21, 22, 23, 25
Wellcome Library, 135, 136
Wills, 52, 54, 57, 63, 64, 65, 84, 85, 139
Women Servants Duty, 85
World War I, 16, 122, 124, 142

Yeomen, 8, 62

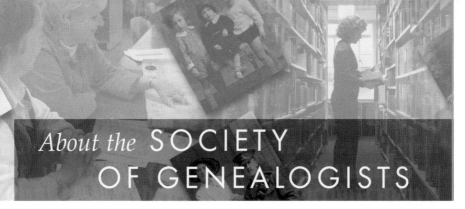

About the SOCIETY OF GENEALOGISTS

Founded in 1911 the Society of Genealogists (SoG) is Britain's premier family history organisation. The Society maintains a splendid genealogical library and education centre in Clerkenwell.

The Society's collections are particularly valuable for research before the start of civil registration of births marriages and deaths in 1837 but there is plenty for the beginner too. Anyone starting their family history can use the online census indexes or look for entries in birth, death and marriage online indexes in the free open community access area.

The Library contains Britain's largest collection of parish register copies, indexes and transcripts and many nonconformist registers. Most cover the period from the sixteenth century to 1837. Along with registers, the library holds local histories, copies of churchyard gravestone inscriptions, poll books, trade directories, census indexes and a wealth of information about the parishes where our ancestors lived.

Unique indexes include Boyd's Marriage Index with more than 7 million names compiled from 4300 churches between 1538-1837 and the Bernau Index with references to 4.5 million names in Chancery and other court proceedings. Also available are indexes of wills and marriage licences, and of apprentices and masters (1710-1774). Over the years the Society has rescued and made available records discarded by government departments and institutions but of great interest to family historians. These include records from the Bank of England, Trinity House and information on teachers and civil servants.

Boyd's and other unique databases are published on line on **www.findmypast.com** and on the Society's own website **www.sog.org.uk**. There is free access to these and many other genealogical sites within the Library's Internet suite.

The Society is the ideal place to discover if a family history has already been researched with its huge collection of unique manuscript notes, extensive collections of past research and printed and unpublished family histories. If you expect to be carrying out family history research in the British Isles then membership is very worthwhile although non-members can use the library for a small search fee.

The Society of Genealogists is an educational charity. It holds study days, lectures, tutorials and evening classes and speakers from the Society regularly speak to groups around the country. The SoG runs workshops demonstrating computer programs of use to family historians. A diary of events and booking forms are available from the Society on 020 7553 3290 or on the website **www.sog.org.uk** .

Members enjoy free access to the Library, certain borrowing rights, free copies of the quarterly *Genealogists' Magazine* and various discounts of publications, courses, postal searches along with free access to data on the members' area of our website.

More details about the Society can be found on its extensive website at **www.sog.org.uk**

For a free Membership Pack contact the Society at:

14 Charterhouse Buildings,
Goswell Road,
London EC1M 7BA.
Telephone: 020 7553 3291
Fax: 020 7250 1800

The Society is always happy to help with enquiries and the following contacts may be of assistance.

Library & shop hours:

Monday	Closed
Tuesday	10am - 6pm
Wednesday	10am - 6pm
Thursday	10am - 8pm
Friday	Closed
Saturday	10am - 6pm
Sunday	Closed

Contacts:

Membership
Tel: 020 7553 3291
Email: membership@sog.org.uk

Lectures & courses
Tel: 020 7553 3290
Email: events@sog.org.uk

Family history advice line
Tel: 020 7490 8911
See website for availability